Field Guide to the Global Economy

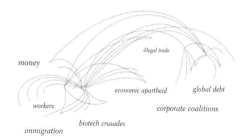

money

illegal trade

economic apartheid

global debt

workers

corporate coalitions

biotech crusades

immigration

Field Guide to the Global Economy

REVISED and UPDATED

SARAH ANDERSON AND
JOHN CAVANAGH WITH THEA LEE

and the Institute for Policy Studies

THE NEW PRESS

Published in the United States by The New Press, New York
Distributed by W. W. Norton & Company, Inc., New York

Library of Congress Cataloging-in-Publication Data

Anderson, Sarah (Sarah Denny)
Field guide to the global economy / Sarah Anderson and John Cavanagh
with Thea Lee; and the Institute for Policy Studies.—Rev. ed.
   p.   cm.
Includes bibliographical references and index.
ISBN 1-56584-956-6 (pbk.)
1. International trade—Handbooks, manuals, etc. 2. Investments,
Foreign—Handbooks, manuals, etc. 3. International finance—Handbooks,
manuals, etc. 4. International business enterprises—Handbooks,
manuals, etc. 5. Social responsibility of business—Handbooks, manuals, etc.
6. International economic relations—Handbooks, manuals, etc. 7. Globalization—
Economic aspects—Handbooks, manuals, etc. I. Cavanagh, John. 1944–
II. Lee, Thea. III. Institute for Policy Studies. IV. Title.

HF1379.A697 2005
658.8′4—dc22

                                                          2004064975

The New Press was established in 1990 as a not-for-profit alternative
to the large, commercial publishing houses currently dominating
the book publishing industry. The New Press operates in the public
interest rather than for private gain, and is committed to publishing,
in innovative ways, works of educational, cultural, and community
value that are often deemed insufficiently profitable.

www.thenewpress.com

Printed in Canada
9 8 7 6 5 4 3 2

Contents

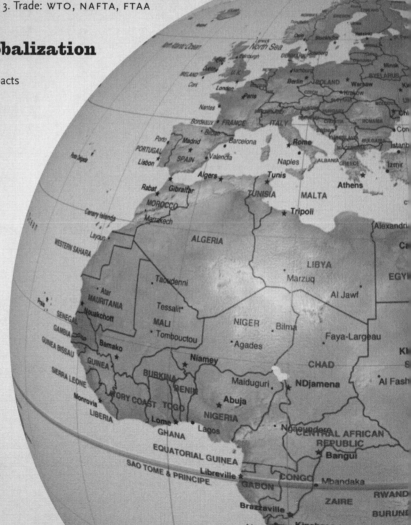

FOREWORD
Barbara Ehrenreich

Watch the commercials on prime time CNN and you'll see enticing images of globalization. Slender yuppies of both sexes stride from airplanes into conference rooms in London or Zurich. Executives in company headquarters confer by computer with engineers in Frankfurt or bankers in Hong Kong, agonizing over how best to preserve the rain forests or develop a life-saving new drug. Cell phones dialed in muddy backwaters of the Southern Hemisphere ring in elegant corner offices. Investments zip through modems at the speed of light. On our television screens, the tantalizing visual clichés flash by one after another—the Eiffel Tower, the Taj Mahal, palm-lined beaches, locals dancing in native costume. We are all connected now, is the message, in one big vibrant, pulsing, global adventure.

There are other, not so pretty images of globalization that seldom appear on television. While the corporate managers fly business class from one financial capital to another, laborers risk their lives sneaking across borders in search of a few dollars more a day in pay. While executives plot corporate strategy over room-service meals, teen-aged girls stitch garments and assemble toys for twelve-hour shifts in airless sweatshops. In this far less glamorous stratum of the global economy, Brazilian and Philippine villages are destroyed by logging companies, while towns in Michigan and Ohio are wiped out by downsizing and plant relocations. You won't find many commercials set around the maquiladoras of northern Mexico or the ramshackle factories of Mumbai, India, where globalization means anxiety, long hours of hard work, and shantytowns with open sewers.

The *Field Guide to the Global Economy* connects the dots between these two worlds of globalization. The problem, according to the authors, is not so much that the world is so tightly linked now—by trade, investments, and high-speed telecommunications—but that the links converge in such a small number of hands. There are 193 nations in the world, many of them ostensibly democratic, but most of them are dwarfed by the corporations that alone decide what will be produced, and where, and how much people will be paid to do the work. In effect, these multinational enterprises have become a kind of covert world government—motivated solely by profit and unaccountable to any citizenry. Only a small group of humans on the planet, roughly overlapping the world's 587-member billionaire's club, rule the global economy. And wherever globalization impinges, inequality deepens. From Mexico to Japan, the rich are getting richer while the poor are becoming more desperate and numerous.

The solution does not lie in a retreat to nationalism and rigid protectionism, or in hermetically sealed economies like that of North Korea. Potentially, globalization could lead to a safer, more peaceful and—who knows?—more interesting world, if, for example, international trade agreements were designed to promote human rights and preserve cultural diversity, instead of just to ease the accumulation of wealth by those who already have more than they know what to do with. But that would be a very different kind of globalization, one in which people who are not "players"—investors or executives—also have a voice.

There's only one way to get there, and it's through even more connectedness, this time among the millions of people at the grubby end of the global economy: labor unions in Mexico linking up with religious groups in Europe; students in California protesting on behalf of workers in Vietnam; women's groups in Massachusetts exchanging information about pharmaceuticals with their counterparts in India or Peru. What you get, as the grassroots networks expand and link up across national boundaries, is something far more exciting than the dash for profits glorified on CNN commercials. It's called solidarity, which is an old-fashioned word for the love between people who may never meet each other, but share a vision of justice and democracy and are willing to support each other in the struggle to achieve it. This is our adventure for the new millennium—recapturing the global economy from its corporate hijackers. Don't be left out.

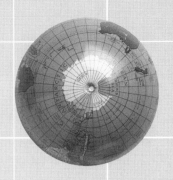
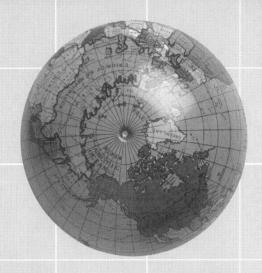

INTRODUCTION
Corporate Globalization

Most of what we eat, drink, wear, drive, smoke, and watch is the product of firms that are now global in their operations. Once wedded to local communities, many of these firms now operate in dozens of countries on all continents save Antarctica. Increasing numbers are owned by shareholders in many different countries. The revenues of these privately owned giants rival the gross national product of many countries.

For those consumers who can afford their wares, these firms offer a dazzling array of goods and services around the world. They are also moving trillions of dollars across borders at lightning speed. Their power over our lives, our planet, and our democratic institutions has never been greater.

Indeed, most governments around the world have facilitated corporate-led globalization by pursuing policies that enhance the ability of corporations to move their products, money, and factories around the globe more quickly and with less impediment from regulations. New and proposed regional and global trade and investment deals aim to lift even further the remaining economic barriers across borders.

1

Yet a powerful backlash has been gaining strength in dozens of countries. Debates rage around the world as to whether such corporate-driven globalization helps or hinders the aspirations of the majority of people on earth. The debates are erupting across college campuses, in labor unions, church basements, parliaments, and city halls, and at millions of dinner tables around the world. This is a healthy development because for decades government policy around the global economy was shaped by a few people, many from the corporate sector, who were quite insulated from the public.

In these debates, those promoting an acceleration of globalization point to the benefits to consumers and workers who find jobs in global factories. Those who make up what is often referred to as a growing "backlash against globalization" point to adverse impacts on equality, natural resources, work, food, communities, culture, and even democracy. And, since the emergence of what we call the "global financial casino" in the late 1990s, millions of people are increasingly anxious about financial crises in one region spreading like wildfire to other countries with devastating economic and environmental consequences.

In the United States, polls show that those opposed to current "pro-globalization" policies outnumber those in favor. A 2004 survey by the University of Maryland showed that fewer than 20 percent of Americans think that the United States should actively promote globalization, while a majority believed that globalization was bad for American workers.[1] Likewise, in many developing countries, trade and investment liberalization has sparked passionate protests, from riots in Indonesia to the toppling of a president in Bolivia.

This book is structured to help nurture both the debates around the global economy and the actions that people take to get involved. It does this by:

- 🌐 **sketching out the history and status of global flows of goods and services, money, and people**
- 🌐 **explaining what is new about globalization today**
- 🌐 **addressing ten common claims of globalization backers**
- 🌐 **describing the major institutions and policies driving globalization**
- 🌐 **highlighting people's efforts to stop, slow down, or change the course of globalization.**

We hope this book will enrich your discussions with friends, colleagues, and family members. For those of you who are moved to act, we end the book with a list of resources that will guide you to some of the more dynamic groups around the world grappling with the global economy.

money

biotech cru

workers

immigration

I. What *Is* Economic Globalization?

Economic globalization consists of the flows of goods and services, capital, and people across national borders. Although globalization has occurred for centuries in each of these realms, it is going through a period of rapid change. Understanding the dynamics of today's global economy requires some knowledge of what came before.

illegal trade

global debt

corporate coalitions

des   *economic apartheid*

History

PRE-1492

Prior to the time of Columbus, most economic activity in the world was highly localized. People ate, drank, worked, and used products that in large part came from close to home. Goods or people from other lands were rare and came from one of three sources:

1. ARMIES: From Alexander the Great to Attila the Hun to the Crusades, armies covered vast distances in pursuit of conquest. Many returned home with plundered goods and slaves from the conquered lands.

2. TRAVELERS AND EXPLORERS: From the Vikings to Marco Polo, people traveled great distances to reach new worlds, often bringing home exotic foods, spices, crafts, and other riches. Indeed, during the early fifteenth century, a Ming Dynasty Chinese emperor built a vast fleet that sailed as far as East Africa, returning with zebras, giraffes, and other live animals.[1]

3. TRADERS: For hundreds of years Chinese and Arab traders plied routes across Asia, the Middle East, and Northern Africa.

Despite these early forays over the millennia, the expense, danger, and uncertainty of long trips limited exchanges, and most people remained untouched by events in other lands. All of this was to change with the onset of what our history books have called the Age of Exploration.

1492—1945 Empire and the Colonial Division of Labor[2]

Columbus did more than sail into the Western Hemisphere in a mistaken quest for an eastern route to the riches of "the Indies." By introducing sugar, oranges, and other products into the hemisphere and by beginning the large-scale extraction of its gold and other minerals, he and other "explorers" began the transformation of who does what in which part of the world. Their behavior toward natives was vicious, treating the Indians "not as beasts, for beasts are treated properly at times, but like the excrement in a public square," according to Friar Bartolomé de las Casas, who accompanied Columbus on his first voyage and later became bishop of Chiapas, Mexico.

Beginning in the late fifteenth century, European powers financed explorations to what would become known as Africa, Asia, and the Western Hemisphere. Within decades, explorations turned to conquest, and colonial authorities directed movements of goods, capital, and people into a new colonial division of labor, some of which persists today. During these four and a half centuries, Spain, Portugal, England, France, the Netherlands, Belgium, Germany, Italy, and later the United States and Japan rearranged economic activity in much of Asia, Africa, and Latin America in the following ways:

MANUFACTURING IN THE RICH COUNTRIES: Colonial authorities sought to undermine indigenous textile manufacturing in the colonies in order to create new markets for the textiles, clothing, and machinery of the colonial powers. Persia, India, the Philippines, and other lands had quite advanced textile centers that were undercut by colonial trade. Cheaper manufactured products from Europe flooded into the colonies which, in turn, were pressed to shift more and more land and people to the production of minerals and agricultural products for export. Only in the United States did the textile industry thrive after colonization.

MINERALS: Columbus sailed west to find gold for Spain. Despite the enslavement and relatively quick annihilation of local populations, little was found in the Caribbean. Much more was soon found in the Aztec and Incan empires of this "new world," and millions of indigenous people died in the mines or from disease spread by the Europeans. As industry flourished in Europe, so too did the demand for copper, tin, bauxite, and other minerals from Latin America and Africa.

AGRICULTURE: To meet the requirements of England's textile mills for cotton and other natural fibers, and the European demand for the luxuries of sugar, coffee, cocoa, tea, and bananas, plantations growing these commodities were carved from forests around the world. Sugar was the greatest early destroyer, beginning with the Portuguese leveling of Brazilian forests in the 1530s and followed by other colonizers across the Caribbean. Hence began the destruction of the world's great tropical rain forests. Colonial trading companies directed much of this traffic until the nineteenth century, when the private Japanese, European, and U.S. firms that are the forbears of some of today's largest global corporations and banks were incorporated.

PEOPLE: Flourishing colonial economic activity in the Caribbean, Brazil, and the southern United States soon exterminated so much of the indigenous population that new labor supplies were needed. Colonial authorities vastly expanded the African slave trade by linking West Africa with the Western Hemisphere. Up to thirteen million Africans were shipped across the Atlantic Ocean between 1444 and 1870, at least two million of them dying in transit of murder, disease, suicide, or malnutrition. While many cut sugar, others sweated in the tobacco, cotton, and rice fields of North America or in the gold and diamond mines of Brazil.

The transformation of most colonies into exporters of one or two minerals or agricultural products twisted those economies into dependence on products over whose price and marketing they had no control.

Since World War II: New Divisions

When World War II broke out across Europe and Asia, the world economy reflected a rather uniform division of labor. In the richer countries of Europe and in the United States, Canada, Japan, and Australia, large corporations sourced the bulk of the world's minerals and agricultural commodities from countries and colonies of Latin America, Africa, and Asia. Today, this basic division has changed radically.

While the richer countries of Europe and North America along with Japan, Australia, and New Zealand still largely export industrial products, among the poorer nations, six groups of countries have emerged:

1. BIG EMERGING MARKETS (in black below). These countries have entered the industrial age to become large-scale manufacturers of a broad range of products. However, they are still poor by many measures, and the global financial crisis of the late 1990s posed a serious setback to the incomes and aspirations of several of these countries.[3]

2. WOULD-BE BEMs (in gray, italics below). These have moved beyond simple assembly of clothing and electronics into a few more diversified and industrial and service sectors.[4]

The Big Emerging Markets (BEMs) and the Would-Be BEMs

3. OPEC NATIONS. These oil-exporting countries have been able to import whole factories for their suddenly affluent populations, but by and large they lack the scientific and engineering expertise to develop their own industrial bases: Venezuela and Indonesia are also OPEC members, but we have listed them in would-be BEMs and BEMs, respectively.

4. FORMER COMMUNIST ECONOMIES. Despite a relatively high state of industrialization, most of the 26 former Soviet bloc nations are finding it difficult to compete for foreign investment with the industrializing enclaves of Asia and Latin America. The rapid shift from socialism to deregulated market economies reliant on external financing left many of these countries vulnerable to the fickleness of the global financial casino. In some cases economic crisis has exacerbated long-standing ethnic tensions.

5. RAW MATERIAL EXPORTERS AND LIGHT MANUFACTURERS.

About 40 countries have little heavy industry beyond assembly, packing, and processing facilities and are suppliers of simple manufactured goods or raw materials for export. Some also earn income from tourism.

6. LEAST DEVELOPED COUNTRIES. About 60 countries, mostly all in Africa, are so poor that their economic connection with the rest of the world is pretty much limited to minimal trade and investment and dwindling foreign aid.

Colonial Division of Labor Still Persists for Many Countries

Among groups five and six, there are forty-seven countries in Latin America, Africa, and Asia that still gain 30 percent or more of their export earnings from one or two agricultural or non-oil mineral products:[5]

Latin America and the Caribbean
Bahamas (shellfish)
Belize (sugar and fruit)
Chile (copper and metal ores)
Cuba (sugar)
Dominica (fruit and stone)
Guadeloupe (sugar and fruit)
Guyana (gold and sugar)
Honduras (fruit and coffee)
Jamaica (metal ores)
Nicaragua (coffee and shellfish)
Panama (fish and fruit)
Paraguay (seeds and cotton)
Saint Lucia (fruit)
Saint Vincent and the Grenadines (fruit and nuts)
Suriname (metal ores)

Africa

Benin (cotton)

Botswana (pearls and stones)

Burkina Faso (cotton)

Burundi (coffee)

Ivory Coast (cocoa and coffee)

Ethiopia (coffee)

Gambia (seeds)

Ghana (cocoa and gold)

Guinea (metal ores)

Kenya (tea and coffee)

Malawi (tobacco)

Mali (gold)

Mauritania (iron ore)

Mozambique (aluminum)

Namibia (pearl and stone)

Niger (uranium)

Reunion (sugar)

Rwanda (coffee)

Senegal (fish and vegetable oil)

Seychelles (fish)

Sierra Leone (precious stones)

Somalia (live animals)

Sudan (cotton and vegetables)

Uganda (coffee and fish)

Zambia (copper)

Zimbabwe (tobacco and cotton)

Asia

Burma (wood and natural gas)

Fiji (sugar and gold)

Maldives (fish)

Papua New Guinea (metal ores)

Solomon Islands (wood)

Tonga (vegetables)

Global Flows Today

This history leaves a world where peoples and countries are increasingly inter-twined. Here is a current snapshot of the state of the three main cross-border flows: goods and services, finance, and people.

A. TRADE IN GOODS AND SERVICES

Through numerous rounds of negotiations or pressure from multilateral agencies, most countries in the world have substantially lifted barriers to trade in goods and services over the last two decades. This "liberalization," combined with new technologies, has made trade increasingly important to the world economy. Between 1980 and 2002, global exports of goods and services grew from 19 to 24 percent of world output."[6]

Exports of Goods and Services (% of World GDP)

Main Goods Traded

Three types of products account for almost one out of every four goods traded.[7]

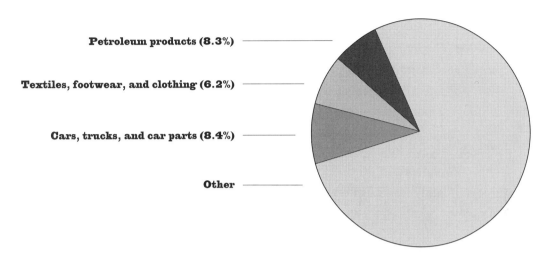

Petroleum products (8.3%)

Textiles, footwear, and clothing (6.2%)

Cars, trucks, and car parts (8.4%)

Other

Main Services Traded

Services account for an increasing share of world trade, particularly for the United States. Between 1980 and 2002, services exports grew from 17 to 21 percent of total global exports, and from 17 to 30 percent of U.S. exports.[8] The leading U.S. service export categories are travel, banking, and insurance, research and development and other industrial services, education and training, computer software and information services, and broadcasting, entertainment, and publishing.[9]

Service Exports as a Percentage of Total Exports

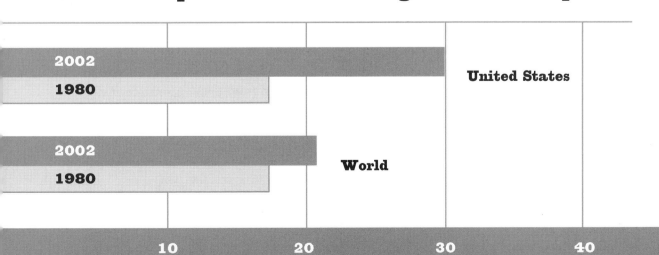

2002

1980

United States

2002

1980

World

10   20   30   40

Illegal Trade

A rising share of global trade does not appear in official trade figures because it is illegal. The biggest components of illegal trade include:

DRUGS The globalization of trade, finance, and communications has made it easier to transport illicit drugs and launder the proceeds. The United Nations has estimated the value of the drug trade to be about $400 billion a year, although experts caution that accurate data are impossible to obtain.[10]

WEAPONS No reliable statistics exist for the illegal trafficking of weapons. However, a report by the Federation of American Scientists claims that the trade in "light" weapons (assault rifles, mortars, grenades, and land mines) has flourished as governments downsized their militaries in the wake of the Cold War and sought cash customers for their arsenals.[11]

PEOPLE The United Nations estimates that four million people per year fall prey to trafficking networks that coerce people into the sex trade, sweatshops, and domestic servitude, generating profits of $5 to $7 billion.[12] These figures include both international trade and "internal" trafficking (e.g., when women are forced to migrate from rural areas to work in urban sex industries), but cross-border trade is clearly on the rise, particularly as increasing numbers of women flee rampant unemployment in former Soviet bloc nations and migrate to the United States, Western Europe, Japan, and elsewhere.

ENDANGERED ANIMALS Interpol estimates that illegal trade in wildlife generates $6 to $10 billion annually.[13] Animals killed by poachers wind up as handbags, medicines, and jewelry. Others caught alive become circus acts and pets for customers all around the world. A World Wildlife Fund investigation of more than 100 traditional medicine stores in the United States and Canada revealed that 50 percent offered illegal substances derived from endangered species such as tiger, rhinoceros, and leopards.[14]

Much of Trade Is Not "Free"

While governments across the globe have lifted numerous barriers to international trade, significant protections remain. In some cases, these mechanisms promote environmental protection, public health, or stable jobs. However, in many cases they are designed not to promote broad social goals but rather to further the narrow interests of the politically powerful. Government interventions in trade can take the form of:

1. IMPORT BARRIERS: Countries use a range of mechanisms to control the flow of imports, including tariffs (taxes on the value of goods for import) and so-called "nontariff barriers," such as outright bans on certain products or quotas to limit the amount of products imported. Often, deep-pocketed corporations are the primary beneficiaries.

2. EXPORT PROMOTION: In the United States, the Export-Import Bank provides loans and loan guarantees to exporting firms, while the Overseas Private Investment Corporation provides insurance to U.S. companies investing abroad. Included in U.S. subsidies are $7 to $8 billion per year related to weapons exports.[15] Worldwide, government agencies subsidize as much as 10 percent of total exports.[16] In addition, governments also commonly fund programs to market products abroad and sometimes subsidize export industries.

3. PROTECTING PATENT MONOPOLIES: The World Trade Organization and other so-called "free trade" agreements include rules on intellectual property that promote monopolies rather than market competition. These rules force governments to adopt U.S.-style patent protections, giving corporations global patent rights that are enforceable by trade sanctions.

B. INTERNATIONAL FINANCIAL FLOWS

For most of history, finance followed and facilitated the production and trade of goods and services. In the late nineteenth and early twentieth centuries, large, privately owned banks emerged in North America, Europe, and Japan. They developed close relationships with large manufacturing firms and financed the activities of those firms around the world. Once established in other countries, they expanded their financing to firms in those nations as well.

Today, in addition to banks, individuals, corporations, and other institutions (e.g., pension funds) are heavily involved in cross-border financial transactions. Since 1980, all international financial flows have accelerated rapidly. This is reflected in the fact that foreign exchange transactions increased 1,355 percent between 1980 and 2001, compared to a 212 percent increase in world merchandise trade.[17] Governments have facilitated this boom by "liberalizing" (lifting barriers to) investment. Liberalizing in this sense might include removing a requirement that large loans get government approval or improving the speed at which funds may be transferred into and out of the country. According to the United Nations, more than 100 countries have passed such laws during the past twenty years.

Financial Flows Outpace Trade Flows

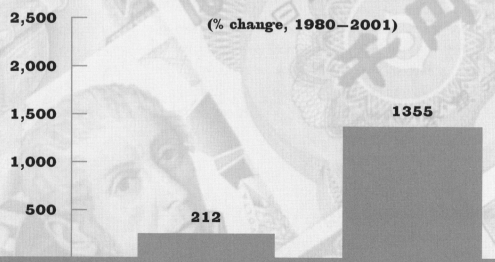

(% change, 1980–2001)

	Value of World Merchandise Trade	Value of Foreign Exchange Transactions
	212	1355

International financial flows include public and private lending:
Public lending comes from governments or from government-funded international financial institutions (e.g., a World Bank loan to the government of Honduras for road construction). This is sometimes called "official" lending. The main sources are the World Bank, the International Monetary Fund, regional development banks, and government aid agencies.

Private financial flows fall into three main categories:

1. FOREIGN DIRECT INVESTMENT (FDI) involves a corporation purchasing a lasting interest in, and degree of influence over, the management of a business in another country (e.g., General Motors and Ford purchasing plants in Mexico).

2. PORTFOLIO INVESTMENT is the cross-border purchase of stocks, bonds, derivatives, and other financial assets. It differs from direct investment in that the investor is generally not seeking management control of local companies (e.g., a U.S. citizen's purchase of a few shares of stock in a German-owned company).

3. DEBT FLOWS include commercial bank loans and bonds (e.g., a Citicorp loan to a Brazilian firm to purchase new equipment).

Financial Flows and the Developing World

Although public lending declined somewhat during the 1990s, private financial flows boomed, particularly into the developing world. Developing countries' share of total foreign direct investment jumped from 20 percent in 1990 to 34 percent in 1995–96.[18] Portfolio investments in the developing world also soared. Some rejoiced over this capital influx, arguing it was the developing world's ticket to prosperity. However, countries soon learned of the dangers of fickle international capital. By 2003, the developing-country share in worldwide foreign direct investment had dropped back to less than 20 percent, with almost 40 percent of that poor-country share going to China alone. Net portfolio flows dropped from $23 billion in 1997 to less than $5 billion in 2002, before rising somewhat in 2003.[19]

Financial Flows to Developing Countries ($ billions)[20]

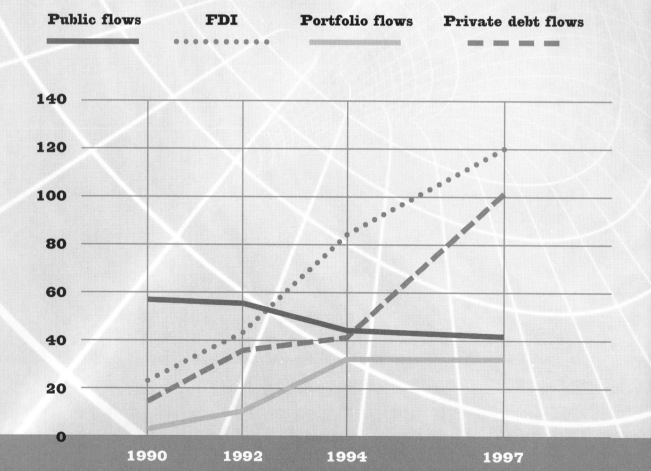

The Chain Reaction of Global Financial Crisis

In mid-1997, jittery Western investors began pulling billions of dollars worth of short-term "hot money" out of Asian countries whose economies were strapped by huge external debts. This began a chain reaction of currency devaluations and stock-market plunges throughout Asia and into other countries, including Russia and Brazil. By the end of 1998, numerous countries showed negative economic growth while their citizens struggled with rampant unemployment, bankruptcies, and in some cases, political unrest. Two years into the crisis, an estimated twenty-seven million workers had lost jobs in the five worst-hit Asian countries alone (Philippines, Indonesia, Malaysia, Thailand, and Korea).[21]

Although these countries have begun to regain what was lost in the crisis, none have attained the GDP levels they enjoyed in the year before the crisis. Compared to 1996, 2002 GDP (in U.S.$) was 30 percent lower in Thailand, 24 percent lower in Indonesia, 8 percent lower in Korea, and 6 percent lower in both Malaysia and the Philippines.[22]

Financial Crisis Struck Lasting Blow to East Asia (GDP, 1996=100)

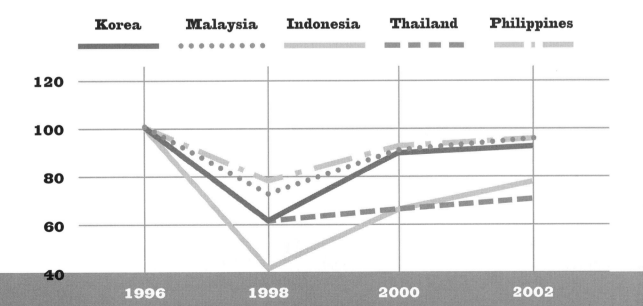

Signs of Financial Crisis   Description

CURRENCY DEVALUATION

When a government increases the amount of its currency it will exchange with other currencies at current exchange rates. For example, three weeks after Brazil devalued in January 1999, the amount of its currency (the real) needed to purchase $1 had jumped from 1.25 to more than 2. Most governments try to avoid sharp devaluations by hiking interest rates and using foreign reserves to buy up the local currency. However, big-time speculators can undermine these efforts by selling off vast amounts of a currency considered to be shaky.

PLUNGING STOCK MARKET

Fearing that the decade-long flood of investment into Asia had created a bubble that was about to burst, investors began selling off stocks with values thought to be inflated. Markets in the United States and elsewhere outside Asia also experienced record one-day plunges. Some analysts said the U.S. market's volatility was partly due to worries that U.S. firms would be hurt by an import surge from desperate Asian nations.

NEGATIVE ECONOMIC GROWTH

The standard measure of growth is the rate of increase in the Gross Domestic Product (GDP), which is the value of goods and services produced by an economy. In 1996, the Asian region had the world's highest GDP growth rates, averaging about 8 percent. But in 1998, many of these former stars fell into the negative. The most dramatic drop was in Indonesia, which had 8 percent GDP growth in 1996 and a 15 percent drop in 1998.

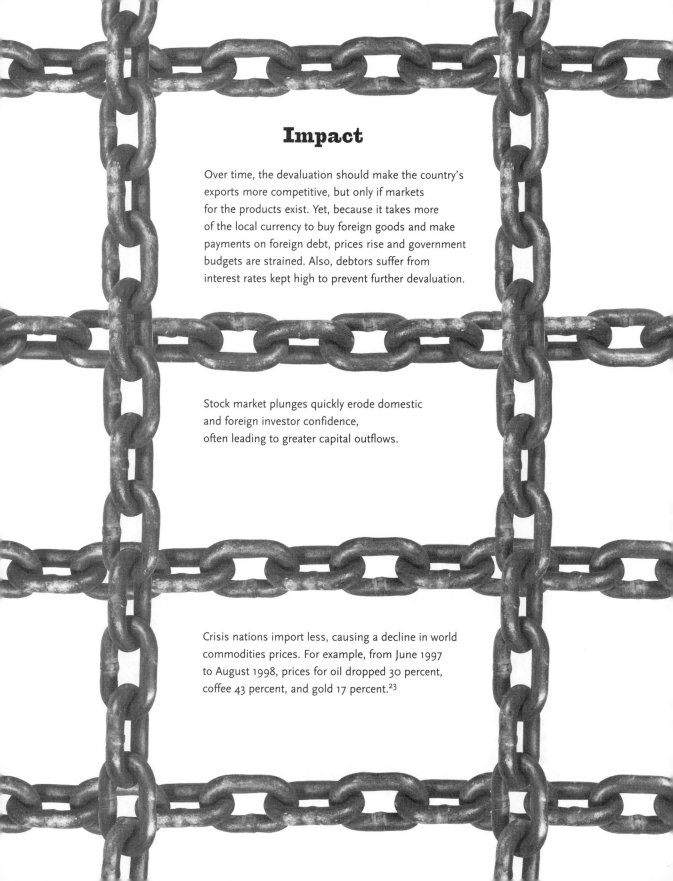

Impact

Over time, the devaluation should make the country's exports more competitive, but only if markets for the products exist. Yet, because it takes more of the local currency to buy foreign goods and make payments on foreign debt, prices rise and government budgets are strained. Also, debtors suffer from interest rates kept high to prevent further devaluation.

Stock market plunges quickly erode domestic and foreign investor confidence, often leading to greater capital outflows.

Crisis nations import less, causing a decline in world commodities prices. For example, from June 1997 to August 1998, prices for oil dropped 30 percent, coffee 43 percent, and gold 17 percent.[23]

Debt Crisis Persists

Large sums of the financial flows to the developing world in recent decades have been loans. In many cases, banks knowingly made loans to dictators who pocketed the money while doing little to help their people. Today, it is the citizens of these nations who bear the burden of repaying these debts to banks in rich nations and to international financial institutions like the World Bank and the International Monetary Fund.

In 1996, the World Bank and International Monetary Fund launched a program to reduce the debts of the most heavily indebted poor countries. However, as of 2004, only thirty-eight countries had qualified, and the World Bank has conceded that many of these countries will not receive sufficient benefits under the program to bring their debts down to manageable levels. Meanwhile, developing-country debt only continues to grow. Between 1995 and 2001, the total foreign debt of developing countries rose from $2.1 trillion to $2.3 trillion.[24]

How debt affects...

POOR COUNTRIES

To keep up with payments on their debt, poor countries often must divert resources from basic services. For example:[25]

1. Zambia spent three times more on debt payments in 2001 and 2002 than on health care, despite the fact that nearly 20 percent of Zambian adults are infected with HIV and the country has the world's highest number of AIDS orphans per capita.

2. Half of Nicaraguans live below the national poverty line, but even after receiving official "debt relief," the government still paid nearly $190 million in payments to rich nations in 2002.

3. Niger, the second poorest country in the world, pays more in debt service than on health, even though life expectancy is only forty-four years and 46 percent of the population is undernourished.

THE UNITED STATES

Meanwhile, the United States and other richer nations are also affected by what has been called the Debt Boomerang:[26]

1. Global Warming: Indebted countries are more likely to plunder their forests for export revenue or to clear forest lands for plantation crops destined for other lands.

2. Job Loss: Debtor countries are less able to purchase U.S. products, resulting in job loss in U.S. export industries.

3. Immigration: Dire economic consequences at home drive millions of people to seek a living in the United States and other rich countries.

C. FLOWS OF PEOPLE

Global flows of people have been nearly as dynamic as flows of goods and capital. International migrants (people who have moved from one country to another) number about 175 million, or about 3 percent of the world's population.[27] People flows are also connected to capital flows because workers follow economic opportunities. Often, these migrants also send money back to their homeland. Immigrants living in the United States sent home an estimated $41.1 billion in 2003, up from $9.2 billion in 1985.[28] Worldwide, such remittances were about $80 billion in 2002, far more than official development aid.[29]

While governments have facilitated the free flow of goods and capital, the trend has been to increase restrictions on the movement of people across borders. The U.S. government refused to discuss migration during negotiations of the North American Free Trade Agreement with Mexico and Canada—except to reduce restrictions for business executives and professionals. In the aftermath of the September 11, 2001 tragedy, legal migration to the United States has been even harder. Due to increased background checks and other new procedures, the backlog of visa applications ballooned from 3.9 million in 2000 to 6.2 million in 2003.[30] Around the globe, many countries have passed laws to make migration easier for highly skilled workers or those with money, but harder for the unskilled and the poor.

Europe's "Open Borders"

One notable exception to the antimigration trend is the internal policy of the European Union. Since 1968, EU citizens have had the right to live and work in any other member state. In some cases, new member countries must go through a transition period before the "open border" policy takes effect. This is currently the case with the new Eastern European members, slated to gain full freedom of movement by the year 2011. Similarly, when Spain and Portugal were negotiating entry in the 1980s, the EU required a five-year transition period. This was in response to widespread fears in the richer member states that Spanish and Portuguese workers would flood northward as soon as borders were lifted. To reduce migration pressures, the EU funneled significant financial and other assistance into the poorer countries that helped lift up living standards in Portugal and Spain. Thus, after borders were lifted in 1991, outmigration was but a trickle. In fact, many Spaniards and Portuguese who had already been living and working in Germany and France returned home to take advantage of new employment opportunities. An increasing number of Latin American leaders argue that a similar approach is needed in the Western Hemisphere.

The EU helped Spain and Portugal Narrow the Economic Gap with their Neighbors...

Per capita income as a percentage of the EU average[31]

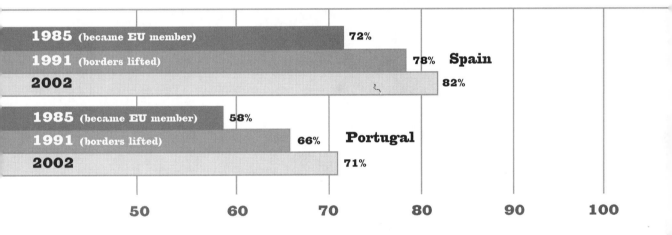

...Making Migration Pressures Negligible

Net migration (per 1,000 inhabitants)[32]

	1991	1992	1993	1994	1995
Spain	0.8	0.7	0.8	0.7	0.9
Portugal	7.2	−1.0	1.0	2.0	2.5

II. What's *New* About the Global Economy?

Many people ask whether economic globalization is really that new
or different. Although globalization has been around for several centuries,
at least eight aspects of it are new.

A. HI-TECH GLOBAL ASSEMBLY LINE

Because of trade and investment liberalization (combined with improved communication and transportation technology), companies today can set up manufacturing plants wherever the costs are lowest. The expense of coordinating such far-flung operations is commonly outweighed by savings in wages, taxes, and the cost of conforming to environmental and other regulations. In 2002, of the 31 million employees of U.S.-based global corporations, 27 percent were working overseas through majority-owned foreign affiliates, up from 21 percent in 1988.[1] This figure represents only a fraction of the jobs shifted out of the United States, since firms are increasingly using overseas subcontractors, for which employment data are not available.

Percentage of U.S. Global Firm Workforce Employed at Foreign Affiliates

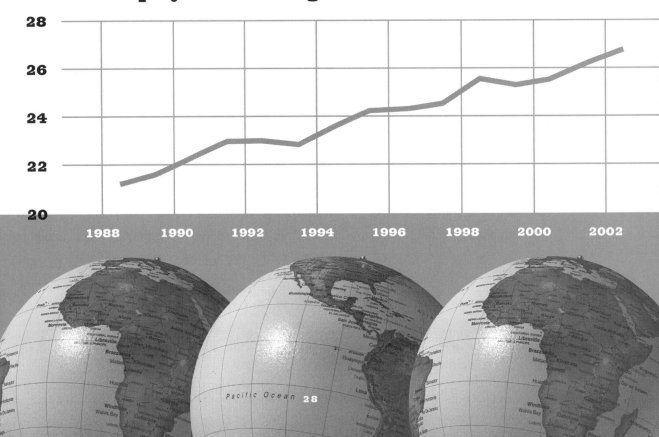

A global assembly line for certain products is not new. As long ago as the 1970s, certain labor-intensive processes such as sewing apparel and assembling electronic goods were shipped to factories in Asia, the Caribbean, and the U.S.–Mexico border. A workforce made up largely of women workers, often denied basic rights, assembled imported components for export abroad. What is new is that a number of poorer countries, led by China and Mexico, now have the infrastructure to house practically any industrial operation—including production of high-tech, capital-intensive products such as automobiles and aircraft. For example, Ford, Boeing, and other global corporations have set up state-of-the-art manufacturing plants in countries where wages and other costs are kept extremely low through repression.

Trading Inside the Corporate Family

One result of the international spread of production is that a large share of world trade is not between countries but between one part of a global firm and an affiliate of that same firm. For example, General Electric ships machinery parts to its own subsidiary in Nuevo Laredo, Mexico, for assembly. Intrafirm trade associated with internationally fragmented production has increased significantly. Between 1982 and 1999, the percentage of exports by U.S.-based global firms to their foreign affiliates that were "intermediate goods" (parts for further manufacture) increased from 15 to 25 percent.[2]

TAX LOOPHOLE

This type of trade offers firms the opportunity to minimize taxes by setting its internal prices in order to maximize losses for subsidiaries in countries with high tax rates and maximize profits in tax havens. This type of accounting chicanery is known as "transfer pricing."

OPPOSITE OF FREE TRADE

It is often argued that one of the benefits of free trade is increased competition—that is, independent firms competing to keep prices low and quality high. But as global corporations essentially trade with themselves, such benefits are seldom passed on to consumers.

B. HIGH TIDE IN THE GLOBAL LABOR POOL

The corporate spread of global assembly lines means that production workers based in richer countries are placed in competition in a global labor pool that includes workers from countries where wages are low and, in most cases, labor-rights protections are weak.

1975 The top fifteen exporters of manufactured goods in 1975 were almost all richer countries with only slight wage differentials. Of those for which wage data were available, the highest average manufacturing wage (Sweden, $7.18 per hour) was less than two and a half times the lowest average wage (Japan, $3).[3]

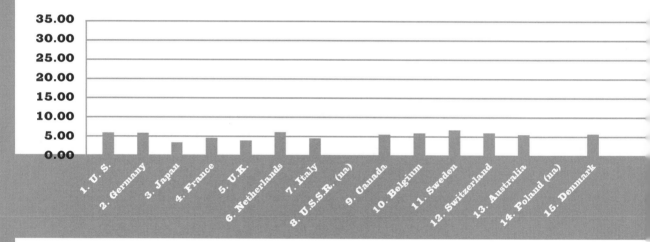

2002 Over the past two and a half decades, the picture has changed dramatically, as a number of low-wage nations joined the world's top exporters. In 2002, the ratio between the highest wage (Germany, $24.31) and lowest (China, $0.90) was 27 to 1.

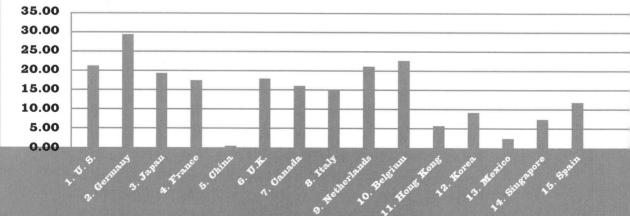

C. CHINA CHALLENGE

China's reemergence as a leading global economic power is perhaps the most dramatic development in the past two decades. The world's most populous nation has transformed from an insulated socialist economy to an export power-house and magnet for foreign capital. Although the Chinese government main-tains a strong role in the economy, the impact of market reforms thus far has been dramatic. In 2003, China became the world's largest net recipient of foreign direct investment, with $53 billion, compared to $40 billion for the United States.[4]

The country has also become an export giant. Between 1980 and 2002, China's exports increased from $14 billion to $365 billion, with more than a third going to the United States. In 2003, the U.S. trade deficit with China ($124 billion) made up one-quarter of the total U.S. trade deficit.

Corporations producing in China for export have benefited from systematic repression that keeps labor costs low. Independent trade unions are banned, meaning workers have little power to demand higher wages. The U.S. govern-ment estimates average Chinese wages to be about 90 cents per hour, but there are documented reports of export workers earning as little as 15 cents per hour.[5] Workers commonly face dangerous working conditions, physical abuse, and nonpayment of wages. They often live crammed twenty to a room in cement-block dormitories, undergoing constant surveillance and intimidation.

China's Total Exports (in U.S.$ billion)

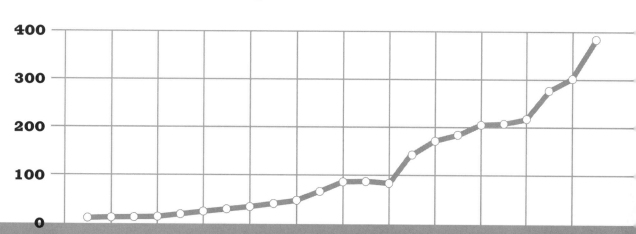

Corporate Profits Outweigh Worker Rights

Research commissioned by the AFL-CIO indicates that labor-rights violations in China artificially depress wages by 47 to 86 percent, and that if the country were to respect basic internationally recognized labor rights, wages would likely increase 90 to 595 percent.[6] However, the U.S. government, supported by U.S. corporations with interests in China, has failed to use its leverage to press for stronger labor-rights protections. The U.S. government didn't even raise the matter in negotiations over China's 2001 entry into the World Trade Organization.

Membership in the global trade body expanded Chinese exporters' access to world markets. In 2005, they are expected to gain a further boost from the phase-out of global textile and apparel quotas. This will throw garment workers in other developing countries, as well as industrialized nations, in open competition with China's rock-bottom wages and repressive labor conditions. The World Bank predicts that as a result, China's share of world garment exports will jump from 20 percent in 2003 to 50 percent by 2010.[7] China's edge is no longer limited to low-skill industries. One sign of the country's rising technological sophistication: In 2003, China exported three times as much in computer and computer parts to the United States as it did footwear.[8]

Major U.S. Corporate Interests in China

Boeing: In order to sell aircraft to the Chinese government, Boeing agreed to provide training and other assistance to help China develop its own aerospace industry. As of 2004, more than 3,300 Boeing airplanes included major parts and assemblies built in China.[9]

Wal-Mart: If Wal-Mart were an independent nation, it would rank as China's fifth-largest export market. The firm's purchases of Chinese-made products totaled $15 billion in 2003. It also operates thirty-five stores in China.[10]

General Motors: GM has invested more than $2 billion since 1998 in joint ventures that produce cars in China, and plans to spend an additional $3 billion between 2004 and 2007.[11]

Ford: Ford aims to buy at least $1 billion in China-produced parts per year for use outside the country.[12] Operates a joint venture auto plant and plans to invest an additional $1 to $1.5 billion in the country in the next few years, expanding output sevenfold.[13]

General Electric: GE aims to purchase $5 billion in China-produced goods in 2005 and is poised to enter the country's consumer and commercial finance market as China lifts restrictions on foreign investment in the sector in coming years.[14]

Coca-Cola: Coca-Cola has twenty-eight bottling plants in China, producing soft drinks that make up 35 percent of the national market.[15]

D. OUTSOURCING OF SERVICE JOBS

"Don't worry; they'll get better jobs in the service sector." During the last three decades of the twentieth century, this was the mantra of most government and business leaders when corporations transferred U.S. auto or apparel jobs to Mexico or China. That line doesn't work anymore, since U.S. firms have started shifting a wide range of service jobs as well, from high-skill computer programming to entry-level call center jobs, to India and other lower-wage nations.

The trend toward foreign outsourcing of service jobs is an extension of a long-standing practice of cutting costs by subcontracting parts of business operations to non-union shops within the United States. The practice has gone global in part because of technological changes. Massive amounts of information can now be transmitted across the world at low cost, making geographic distances less important. International financial institutions and trade agreements have also facilitated the trend by promoting investment liberalization and privatization of public services, creating new opportunities for U.S. corporations in overseas markets.

U.S. Occupations at Risk for Outsourcing[16]

Number employed domestically, as of 2001

Medical Transcriptionists	94,090
Diagnostic Support Services	168,240
Paralegals and Legal Assistants	183,550
Business and Financial Support	2,153,480
Computer and Math Professionals	2,825,870
Office support	8,637,900
Computer Operators	177,990
Data Entry Keyers	405,000
TOTAL AT RISK	14,063,130
PERCENT OF TOTAL WORKFORCE	11.0%

Although the number of jobs lost so far is small relative to the total workforce, these layoffs have a huge impact on the affected communities, and the potential for white-collar jobs to be outsourced is deeply unsettling for many American workers. In addition to job cuts, service workers now must also contend with the enhanced power of highly mobile, increasingly unregulated global firms to bargain down U.S. wages and working conditions by threatening to move jobs elsewhere.

India is by far the leading developing-country destination for U.S. service-sector outsourcing. In 2004, U.S. firms accounted for more than two-thirds of the country's $12.5 billion annual business in international software and business-support services. Already employing about 1 million people, India's international service market is expected to quadruple by 2008.[17] Given a lack of other economic opportunities, Indian workers are often eager to secure new jobs catering to the U.S. market. However, they face the nagging fear that these jobs may evaporate as soon as firms can find lower costs elsewhere. Meanwhile, among the Indian poor who have not benefited from the global service sector, resentment is rising, and poorer voters were seen as key to the defeat of the ruling party in India's 2004 national elections.

Hourly Wages: U.S. Versus Indian Service Jobs (U.S.$)[18]

	U.S.	INDIA
Telephone Operator	12.57	$1
Health Record Technologists/ Medical Transcriptionists	13.17	1.50–2.00
Payroll Clerk	15.17	1.50–2.00
Legal Assistant/Paralegal	17.86	6.00–8.00
Accountant	23.35	6.00–15.00
Financial Researcher/Analyst	33.00–35.00	6.00–15.00

E. PLANET WAL-MARS

For most of the past half century, car and petroleum companies dominated the top spots of the world's largest corporations. In recent years, however, a retailer with modest roots in Arkansas has charged ahead of all of them, growing to planetary proportions. As writer Barbara Ehrenreich puts it, efforts to rein in that company "could be the central battle of the twenty-first century: Earth people versus the Wal-Martians." [19]

Wal-Mart is No. 1 in:
Global sales ($256.3 billion in 2003)
Global employment (1,500,000)
U.S. imports from China ($15 billion in 2003)
Retail sales in Mexico (7 percent of total)

Wal-Mart has become number one by exploiting workers the world over, accelerating the global "race to the bottom" in wages and working conditions.

American Wal-Mart Workers: Despite all the happy faces in their TV ads, the company's workers, called "associates," receive terrible pay. Average wages in 2004 were about $9 per hour for full-time workers and $8 per hour for the 45 percent of Wal-Mart employees who work less than forty-five weeks per year. Compensation is so stingy that many Wal-Mart workers must rely on government health care, food, housing, and other aid. A study by Congressional Democratic staff estimated that Wal-Mart workers receive on average $2,103 per year in federal subsidies alone.[20]

The company is also a notorious union-buster. In the United States, the only Wal-Mart workers to ever win union recognition were meat cutters at a Texas store. The company promptly announced that it was closing its meat-cutting operations. In August 2004, workers at a Wal-Mart in Quebec, Canada, gained union certification, but still faced a challenge in gaining a collective agreement.

Wal-Mart Suppliers: Because of its dominance in the global marketplace, Wal-Mart has tremendous power to squeeze its more than 65,000 suppliers.[21] It demands that even venerable brands like Vlasic Pickles and Levi's cut costs to the bone, and sometimes deeper. In the Levi's case, getting a Wal-Mart contract boosted profits but forced the firm to close its remaining U.S. and Canadian factories in search of cheaper labor.[22]

Wal-Mart Workers Abroad: Developing-country workers bear the brunt of Wal-Mart's vice grip on suppliers. A study by the National Labor Committee found that workers in China's Guangdong Province who made toys for Wal-Mart toiled as much as 130 hours per week for wages averaging 16.5 cents per hour (below the minimum wage) and no health insurance.[23] A study by Oxfam documented that Wal-Mart's use of exploited labor in China has put further downward pressure on wages and working conditions at their supplier factories throughout the developing world.[24] Wal-Mart's determination to be union-free extended to its retail stores in China, where until late 2004 it banned the union controlled by the governing Communist Party, despite assurances that the union "wouldn't help workers struggle for better pay."[25]

Communities: When Wal-Mart comes to town, locally owned businesses must struggle to compete with "everyday low prices." A widely cited study by Iowa State University documented that rural communities (the focus of Wal-Mart's initial expansion) lost up to 47 percent of their retail trade ten years after the discount giant's arrival.[26] There is less research on the impacts on Wal-Mart's new frontier: urban neighborhoods. However, a University of Illinois study concluded that a Wal-Mart coming to a Chicago neighborhood would likely result in a net job decrease as other retailers lose business. Despite these costs, state and local governments have spent more than $1 billion in subsidies to attract Wal-Marts to their communities.[27]

F. OPEN DOORS TO FOREIGN DIRECT INVESTMENT

Until recently, many nations placed numerous restrictions on foreign investment. Much of the developing world excluded investment in what they considered "strategic" sectors: mining, petroleum, banking, insurance, and culture. The World Bank and International Monetary Fund have pushed countries to dismantle these restrictions since the early 1980s. One result has been a flurry of government "privatization" of state-owned enterprises, with most buyers coming from the ranks of global corporations. In the 1990s, trade negotiations began to further limit the ability of governments to maintain many of these controls. The "trade-related investment measures" (TRIMS) section of the World Trade Organization prohibits countries from imposing certain requirements on foreign investors, such as demanding that they use local inputs and workers. The North American Free Trade Agreement (NAFTA) went much further to break down investment barriers and has been considered a model by U.S. officials negotiating other agreements (see Chapter IV). In addition, dozens of countries have signed bilateral investment treaties with rules similar to those in NAFTA.

**Interested investors can browse magazine ads, like these from
Latin Trade, for bargains on buying up state-owned enterprise.**

ector	Project	Description	Deadline	Institution	Contact	Phone	Fax
IL SYSTEM							
ızil	Concession of FEPASA	30 year concession for the operation and maintenance of the rail network. Bids started in July 1998.	Pending	BNDES	Jose Pio Borges	[55](21)277.7059	[55](21)533.1
ombia	Pacific Rail Network	30 year concession for the repair, operation and maintenance of the rail network. It includes the Buenaventura- Felisa and the Zarzal-Tebaida branch sectors.	8/13/98	Ferrovias	Julian Palacio	[57](1)285.0957	[57](1)288.36
sta Rica	Atlantic Railway Concession	25 year concession for the rehabilitation, operation and maintenance of the Atlantic railway sector. Bids opened in February 1998.	Pending	Incofer	Rolando Rivera	[506]256.0713	[506]222.699
iguay	Tren de la Costa	Concession for the design, construction and operation of a railway between Montevideo and El Pinar.	Pending	AFE	Victor Vaillant	[598](2)924-0815	N/A
)ADS							
lombia	Malla vial del Valle	Concession for the construction, repair and the maintenance of the highways in Cauca and Valle del	8/20/98	INVIAS	Javier Toro	[57](1)222.3816	[57](1)222.37

G. GLOBAL FINANCIAL CASINO

Money now moves around the world at a speed that defies and baffles government regulators. This acceleration was caused by policies to "liberalize" (lift barriers to) capital flows, combined with advancements in information technology. Although flows of money across borders have slowed somewhat since their peak in the late 1990s, they still average $1.2 trillion per day—twice what they were in 1989.[28] Only one to two percent of these transactions are related to trade or foreign direct investment. The remainder is for speculation or short-term investments that are subject to rapid flight when investors' perceptions change.[29]

After Mexico suffered a rapid exodus of capital in late 1994, the International Monetary Fund and other global agencies claimed that they had set in place new safeguards to prevent a repeat. Yet, the Fund and the U.S. Treasury Department continued to pressure nations to remove remaining restrictions on capital inflows and outflows. Nobel economist Joseph Stiglitz believes this was the "single most important factor" leading to the global financial crisis that erupted in Asia in the late 1990s.[30]

Daily International Foreign Exchange Transactions (in U.S.$ trillions)

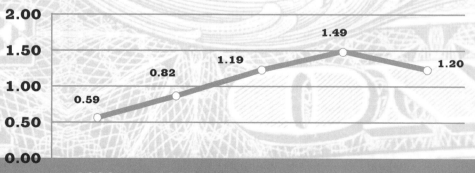

Year	Value
1989	0.59
1992	0.82
1995	1.19
1997	1.49
2001	1.20

H. BIOTECH CRUSADES [31]

For 12,000 years, farmers have survived by saving, breeding, and exchanging seeds for next year's harvest. The health and sustenance of billions of the world's poor depends on the biological diversity that has evolved from these processes.

Today, the rise of a new industry called "biotechnology" threatens to kill that diversity. Chemical, agribusiness, and pharmaceutical companies have manipulated genetic codes to create inventions that they claim improve upon Mother Nature. In agriculture, corporations are aggressively marketing genetically engineered seeds that are designed to produce higher yields but have raised a number of concerns:

- **MONOPOLIES:** Biotech firms are using strong-arm tactics to gain even more control over the world's food supply and wipe out biodiversity.

- **ENVIRONMENT:** Genetically engineered crops are largely untested and could spread pesticide-resistant genes to weeds.

- **HEALTH:** Little research has been done on the effects of eating genetically engineered crops.

U.S.-based Monsanto is the most aggressive champion of biotechnology in agriculture. In 2003, the firm's genetically modified soybean, corn, cotton, and canola seeds accounted for 90 percent of acres worldwide planted with biotech seeds.[32] The company also produces Roundup, the world's top-selling herbicide, designed for use with Monsanto's genetically modified seeds.

Monsanto claims it takes about a decade and $300 million to develop a successful genetically modified seed. To recoup these costs, the company pressures farmers to buy large quantities each year by making them agree not to replant the seeds in the next season; farmers who do save and replant Monsanto seeds are charged with "seed piracy." One such Monsanto lawsuit targeted a Canadian farmer who claimed that Monsanto's Roundup Ready canola seeds had blown onto his fields. Despite his argument that he had not intentionally planted the seeds, the Canadian Supreme Court ruled in favor of Monsanto in May 2004.

Around the world, organic farmers fear similar problems, since regulations to contain potential genetic pollution are lacking. On the other hand, consumer opposition to biotech food is on the rise (see Chapter V).

III. Globalization Claims

Since the onset of the debate over the North American Free Trade Agreement
(NAFTA) in 1990, the U.S. public, press, and government have engaged
in a lively and often polarized debate over economic globalization.
Almost all participants in the debate agree that the current approach
to globalization produces winners and losers. Yet there are vast differences
in the overall calculations of who wins and who loses. Virtually all leaders
of large U.S. corporations claim that the benefits of such policies
far outweigh the costs. However, polls consistently show that the majority
of Americans are skeptical about the benefits of these policies, and the
U.S. Congress is sharply divided on the issue. The following section addresses
ten common claims of supporters of the current globalization policies.

TRADE AND INVESTMENT LIBERALIZATION = MORE GOOD JOBS

CLAIM #1

Free trade is good for American workers, because when American workers compete on the world stage, American workers win.
—U.S. Trade Representative's office[1]

Current trade policies limit the power of governments everywhere to support high-quality jobs. For example, global trade rules restrict the use of import controls to support key industries and prohibit governments from requiring that foreign investors hire local workers or use local suppliers.

Import Competition

In the United States, trade liberalization has led to a flood of imported manufactured goods. Between 1980 and 2003, the annual U.S. trade deficit in goods rose from $25 billion (less than 1 percent of GDP) to $547 billion (5 percent of GDP).[2] During this same period, U.S. manufacturing employment dropped from 18.7 million to 14.5 million.[3]

Supporters of current trade policies dismiss the charge that the trade deficit has hurt American workers, arguing that job losses are the result of increased automation, not increased imports. However, research by the Economic Policy Institute in Washington, D.C., indicates that the expanded trade deficit is indeed the most important factor. Between 1998 and 2003, a period of particularly sharp decline in manufacturing jobs, the EPI found that the trade imbalance accounted for 59 percent of the drop in manufacturing employment, or about 1.8 million jobs.[4]

U.S. Manufacturing Employment (in thousands)

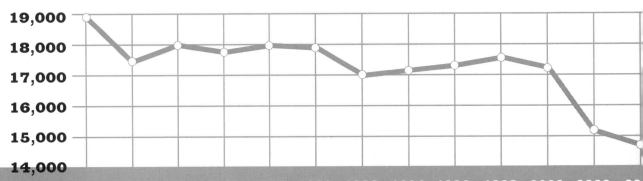

Runaway Jobs

Trade liberalization also increases the incentive for highly mobile global firms to shift production in search of the lowest labor costs. Corporations that manufacture products abroad and export them to the U.S. market face reduced tariffs and fewer... trade barriers.

General Electric has been one of the largest exporters of U.S. jobs to low-wage countries. Between 1986 and 1998, the company cut its U.S. workforce nearly in half, while nearly doubling its foreign operations. In 1999, GE's Mexican factories employed 30,000 workers.[5] That year, GE's CEO at the time, Jack Welch, earned $141 million—two and a half times the pay of his combined Mexican workforce.

Ideally, you'd have every plant you own on a barge. —Jack Welch, former CEO, General Electric[6]

To further cut costs, GE began pressuring its suppliers to move to Mexico as well. In a series of conferences titled "Globalization and Supplier Migration," the company ordered its suppliers to move south of the border. According to notes taken by one participant, "GE set the tone early and succinctly: 'Migrate or be out of business; not a matter of if, just when.'" Not surprisingly, there has been a steady migration of GE suppliers to Mexico and other low-wage countries during the years hence.

New Jobs Are Bad Jobs

The Labor Department reports that only about 26 percent of laid-off manufacturing workers find new jobs that pay as well or better than their old jobs.[7] One explanation is that virtually all the new American jobs being created are in the lower-paying service sector. And the future looks bleak. Of the ten occupations projected to have the largest growth in coming years, five have median pay that is below the poverty line for a family of four.[8]

Projected Top Growth Jobs, 2002–2012

(ranked by number of jobs expected to be created)

	2002 median annual earnings	projected new job creation over 10 years
1. Registered nurses	$48,090	623,000
2. Postsecondary teachers	$49,090	603,000
3. Retail salespersons	$17,710	596,000
4. Customer service representatives	$26,240	460,000
5. Cashiers	$15,420	454,000
6. Food preparation and serving	$14,500	454,000
7. Janitors	$18,250	414,000
8. Managers	$68,210	376,000
9. Waiters	$14,150	367,000
Poverty line for a family of four, 2002	$18,660	

Globalization Blackmail

After a long stagnation, American wages rose slightly in the 1990s, but not nearly as fast as corporate profits. Over the thirteen-year period from 1990 to 2003, real U.S. wages rose a paltry 7 percent on average, compared to a real increase in corporate profits of 103 percent and in CEO pay of 274 percent.[9] Why the disparity? Part of the explanation is that globalization has weakened the power of American workers to fight for better wages and working conditions. A Cornell University study documented threats by U.S. employers to move to low-wage countries in order to fight unions and restrain wages. It found that the frequency of such threats in union organizing drives increased from about 50 percent in the early 1990s to 68 percent in 1999.[10]

FOREIGN OUTSOURCING IS GOOD FOR AMERICAN WORKERS

CLAIM #2

*Outsourcing is just a new way of doing international trade. . . .
More things are tradeable than were tradeable in the past.
And that's a good thing.* —N. Gregory Mankiw, chief economic advisor to President George W. Bush[11]

The accelerated movement of service jobs to low-wage countries has created tremendous insecurity among American workers. Cheerleaders of the practice, however, argue that foreign outsourcing increases efficiency and that companies will turn around and use increased profits to support jobs in the United States.

Outsourcing does indeed increase profits by lowering labor costs. But there is no evidence that this translates into increased American jobs. For example, U.S. software-related jobs, some of the most vulnerable to outsourcing, have been in steady decline, dropping 16 percent between 2001 and 2004, while U.S. imports of software from India have grown significantly.[12]

The possibility of a positive boomerang effect for U.S. workers is increasingly slim, given that more and more developing-country workers rival their U.S. counterparts in education and technological sophistication. Meanwhile, the countries that are the primary destination of outsourced U.S. jobs face uncertain futures. In the short-term they are attracting some jobs. But no one knows how long they will last before highly mobile firms find a better deal elsewhere.

Source: Center for American Progress (www.americanprogress.org).

CLAIM #3

AS TRADE SPURS ECONOMIC GROWTH, GOVERNMENTS INVEST MORE IN THE ENVIRONMENT

An open world trading system contributes to the prosperity of less developed countries and helps them get to the point of mandating and enforcing environmental standards similar to those in the developed world.
—Gene Grossman, Princeton University, whose work was often cited in the NAFTA debate[13]

Developing Country Exports Are Often Based on Resource Plunder

Globalization puts multiple pressures on the environment. Rapid, uncontrolled development of export industries has vastly increased pollution around the world. Some global companies deliberately choose production locations where environmental enforcement is lax. Further, the World Bank and International Monetary Fund pressure countries to pay off loans through increased export earnings. This often means cutting down forests for timber exports or plantation expansion, depleting fishing stocks, or expanding open-pit mines.

Advocates of current globalization policies counter that expanded exports fuel economic growth, which, in turn, gives governments more resources to invest in environmental clean-up. The record, however, suggests otherwise. All four leading exporters in the developing world—China, Mexico, Malaysia, and Brazil—have significant environmental problems linked to export-oriented policies.

CHINA   VALUE OF EXPORTS, 1980–2002: $2.6 trillion
RANK IN DEVELOPING WORLD: 1

China's export-industry boom during the past two decades has contributed
to costly pollution problems.

- At least sixteen of the twenty cities with the world's worst air pollution are in China.
  In 2000 alone, air pollution caused 600,000 premature deaths, 5.5 million cases
  of chronic bronchitis, and 20 million cases of respiratory illness.
- The World Bank has estimated conservatively that air and water pollution reduce
  China's GDP by 3.5 to 8 percent.
- Pollution of farmland causes an estimated annual loss of $1.5 billion worth
  of staple foods.[14]

MEXICO   VALUE OF EXPORTS, 1980–2002: $1.7 trillion
RANK IN DEVELOPING WORLD: 2

Under the North American Free Trade Agreement (NAFTA), Mexico's exports
to the United States have ballooned, but the explosion of foreign-owned export
assembly plants has intensified environmental problems.

- Air pollution from Mexican manufacturing doubled during NAFTA's first four years.[15]
- During the same period, Mexican government investment in environmental protection
  declined in real terms by about 45 percent despite rapid export growth.[16]

MALAYSIA   VALUE OF EXPORTS, 1980–2002: $1.2 trillion
RANK IN DEVELOPING WORLD: 3

To support the country's export-oriented industrial development, Malaysia has destroyed
much of its rainforest. It dominates the international market in tropical logs.[17]

- Indiscriminate logging peaked in the 1980s, but the country lost an additional
  13 percent of its natural forest area in the 1990s.[18]
- Deforestation has led to serious erosion, dumping as much as 60 million tons
  of soil into rivers annually.[19]
- Logging has reduced biodiversity and destroyed the livelihoods of indigenous
  communities that rely on forest products.

BRAZIL   VALUE OF EXPORTS, 1980–2002: $958 billion
RANK IN DEVELOPING WORLD: 4

During the past three decades, Brazilian mahogany exports (valued at $4 billion)
contributed significantly to deforestation in the Amazon. Although the current
government is attempting to control mahogany logging, the world's largest rainforest
continues to be severely threatened by agribusiness.

- 10,000 square miles of the Amazon were razed in 2003, a 40 percent increase over
  2002, largely to grow soybeans for export.[20]
- In 2004, Brazil became the world's largest beef exporter, thanks in part to the fact
  that the number of cattle in the Amazon region more than doubled in 2002.[21]

Globalization Also Threatens the Environment in Developed Countries

BLACKMAIL Mobile corporations can more effectively use threats of moving production elsewhere in order to weaken U.S. environmental regulations. For example, a 2003 California rule limiting air pollution from lawnmowers was gutted under pressure from one company, Briggs & Stratton. The company claimed that if the law went into effect, it would raise production costs so much that the firm would have to shut down its small-engine production plants in the United States. U.S. Congressman Kit Bond (R-MO), whose district is home to a Briggs & Stratton plant, spearheaded an amendment in Congress that preempted the California law. He argued that the antipollution measure would force the firm to "rebuild these facilities in China because they could do it so much more cheaply and use less expensive labor."[22]

PUBLIC HEALTH THREATS Inspections of food imports have not kept pace with increases in trade flows, increasing the risk of getting sick from eating uninspected, contaminated food. In addition, international trade rules prohibit governments from discriminating against products on the basis of how they were produced. This means that foreign producers can use pesticides and other chemicals banned in the United States on products destined for the U.S. market.

LAWS OVERTURNED Environmental regulations are also subject to being challenged under trade rules as "unfair barriers to trade" (see Chapter IV).

PEST INVASION Growth of international trade has increased the number of exotic insects, plants, and animals that enter the United States on imported goods. After habitat loss, the invasion of nonnative species is the second-greatest threat to native American plants and animals and costs the U.S. economy more than $120 billion annually in lost crops, forests, and home infestations.[23]

CLAIM #4

TRADE AND INVESTMENT LIBERALIZATION ARE GOOD FOR THE POOR

Those who protest free trade are no friends of the poor. Those who protest free trade seek to deny them their best hope for escaping poverty. —President George W. Bush[24]

Officials in the U.S. government and the international financial institutions often tout research that supposedly shows that countries that are "globalizers" have made more progress in reducing poverty than those that are not. These claims are extremely distorted because they include among the so-called "globalizer" nations large countries like China and India that have indeed reduced extreme poverty, but not as a result of the types of trade and investment liberalization policies that the U.S. government, World Bank, and IMF have promoted. For example, the Chinese government has applied extensive restrictions on foreign investment and tightly controlled trade flows through quotas and import and export licenses. In fact, the Heritage Foundation, a leading advocate of trade liberalization, gave China the Foundation's lowest possible rating for trade openness in its 2004 Index of Economic Freedom.[25]

Harvard University economist Dani Rodrik has pointed out that overall in the developing world, countries with high import barriers did better in the 1990s than those with low barriers. He argues that openness to the global economy is usually a *result* of economic development—not a *cause* of it.[26]

Likewise, the Center for Economic and Policy Research has documented that economic growth rates in the developing world were actually slower on average during the 1980–2000 period (when most countries were pursuing trade and investment liberalization policies) than they were in the two prior decades.[27]

This record demonstrates that governments should have the flexibility to develop their own economic strategies that reflect national and local priorities and conditions. Nevertheless, international institutions such as the World Bank and International Monetary Fund continue to promote a "one-size-fits-all" formula for prosperity.

Number of Those Living in Poverty Has Increased in the Developing World

Despite more than two decades of reforms in most countries in the world to lift barriers to trade and investment, the number of people living on less than $2 a day has increased in all regions except East Asia.[28]

People Living on Less Than $2 Per Day (in millions U.S.$)		
	1981	2001
South Asia	821	1,059
East Asia and Pacific	1,151	868
China	858	596
Sub-Saharan Africa	288	514
Latin America and Caribbean	99	128
Europe and Central Asia	8	93
Middle East and North Africa	52	70
TOTAL	2,419	2,732
TOTAL, EXCLUDING CHINA	1,561	2,136

Globalization and Rural Poverty

There are many ways that current globalization policies hurt the poor. As detailed in other sections of this book, these policies increase the power of corporations to bargain down wages by pitting workers against one another, put pressure on governments to slash spending for the poor, and contribute to the destruction of natural resources on which many people depend for their livelihoods. But perhaps the most devastating effects have been in the agriculture sector, which employs about 70 percent of the developing world's poor.

1. Import Competition: Trade rules restrict governments' power to place controls on imports, opening the door to cheaper foreign commodities that undercut local farmers.

- In the Indian state of Andhra Pradesh, 2,000 to 3,000 farmers committed suicide between 1998 and 2004. Their economic distress was caused, in part, by trade liberalization that led to a flood of palm oil imports from Southeast Asia.[29]

2. Subsidy Cuts: The World Bank and IMF have pressured developing country governments to slash supports for small producers. This makes it even more difficult for them to compete with imports from rich countries, which are often heavily subsidized.

- In Central America, World Bank and IMF policies have mostly eliminated support for credit, technological assistance, and infrastructure for small farmers. Between 1980 and 2002, the region's agricultural population dropped by 5.5 percent, or more than 2 million.[30]

3. Export Glut: The promotion of export-oriented agriculture has in some cases caused world market prices to crash. For example, the current global coffee crisis is largely attributed to a spike in global supply due to expanded production in Vietnam. In addition, the shift to export crops reduces the availability of food needed for survival.

- An estimated 600,000 coffee workers lost their jobs in Central America alone in 2003.[31]

CLAIM #5

FREE TRADE IS THE CONSUMERS' BEST FRIEND

[Increased trade] spurs innovation among domestic firms while protecting consumers from potential monopolies.
—Daniel Griswold, Cato Institute [32]

That consumers benefit from freer trade is perhaps the most pervasive assertion of globalization supporters. And there is no question that globalization has expanded the variety of goods available in the marketplace. Pristine malls selling the same goods now tower over cityscapes from Manila to Mexico City.

It is also true that roughly a third of U.S. imports come from poorer nations where workers earn a fraction of U.S. wages. Hence, these goods often *enter* the United States at prices far below the price of U.S.-made goods. Yet, a key question is how often firms then *sell* those goods to consumers at lower prices versus how often they hike the prices and keep the benefits of trade for themselves.

Evidence suggests that in sectors of the economy where many small producers compete, such as clothing production, consumers may find that increased trade lowers prices. However, in sectors where a handful of huge global firms dominate the market for a particular product, international trade often does not result in lower prices.

For example, four firms control more than 60 percent of the global market for coffee sold in grocery stores: Altria (formerly Philip Morris) controls about 25 percent; Nestlé, 24 percent; Sara Lee, 7 percent; and Procter and Gamble, 7 percent.[33] Their oligopoly control helps explain why Americans have paid only slightly less for a pound of coffee at the supermarket in spite of a crash in world market prices for coffee beans that has devastated millions of farmers.[34]

No Free Trade Bargains at General Motors

General Motors demonstrates how global firms that dominate a particular industry can monopolize the benefits of international trade. In 1994, GM decided to
expand production of its popular "Suburban" sport utility vehicle. But instead of
investing in its Suburban plant in Janesville, Wisconsin, or adding capacity at
another U.S. plant, the company built a new facility in Silao, Mexico, which began
producing Suburbans for the U.S. market. Yet, as GM's wage bill plummeted, the
price of Suburbans sold in the United States continued to rise.[35]

GM's move to Mexico drastically cut the firm's labor costs ...

Average 1996 wages of workers who make Suburbans:

U.S. $18.96 per hour   Mexico $1.54 per hour

... yet GM did not lower the price of the vehicle

Sticker price of a Suburban:

1994: $21,000–$24,500   1996: $23,500–$31,000

By 1996, GM produced nearly as many Suburbans in Silao, Mexico (80,400),
as in Janesville, Wisconsin (83,000).

GLOBALIZATION LIFTS ALL BOATS

CLAIM #6

Antiglobalization activists are convinced that economic integration has been widening the gap between rich and poor. The best evidence, however, proves them wrong.
—David Dollar and Aart Kraay, World Bank[36]

The official World Bank view for the past two decades has been that trade and investment liberalization helps reduce inequality by increasing economic growth. However, even within the World Bank, there is a growing body of research that shows otherwise.

Inequality Within Countries:

In the first study of world income distribution based on household surveys, World Bank researcher Branko Milanovic found significant increases in inequality in poor countries that lifted barriers to trade and investment.[37] The average income of the poorest 10 percent of the population dropped from 30.7 percent of the national average in 1988 to 23.3 percent in 1998. At the same time, the average income of the richest 10 percent rose from 274.5 percent of the national average to 313.8 percent.[38] The study found that globalization tended to increase inequality most in the poorest countries, where per capita incomes were lower than $5,000–7,000.

Inequality Increase in Trade-Liberalizing Countries

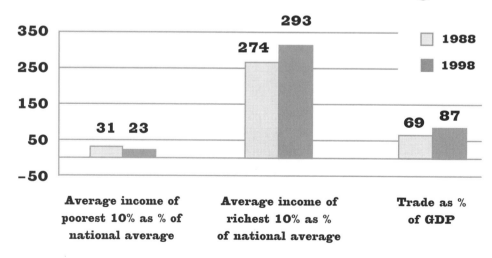

Legend: ☐ 1988 ■ 1998

	1988	1998
Average income of poorest 10% as % of national average	31	23
Average income of richest 10% as % of national average	274	293
Trade as % of GDP	69	87

Another researcher, a former World Bank economist, examined eight alternative measures of inequality and found that seven indicated increased disparity over the past two decades, while the eighth showed no significant change.[39] The World Bank has also documented that in Latin America, where trade and investment liberalization policies are most advanced, not a single country had a significant decline in inequality in the 1990s.[40]

Inequality Between Countries:

The gap in per capita income between the thirty richest and the thirty poorest countries grew from 17 to 1 in 1980 to 27 to 1 in 2002.[41]

Inequality Between Have-Nots and Have-Mores:

In 2003, the wealth of the world's 587 billionaires ($1.9 trillion) was greater than the combined incomes of the poorest half of humanity.[42]

HOW GLOBALIZATION IS PULLING US APART

Dragging the Bottom Down

IN THE UNITED STATES: Workers with no more than a high school diploma earn average wages that are far lower today than they were in the 1970s (adjusted for inflation).[43] Most economists, including some who support current trade policies, attribute as much as 25 percent of the increase in U.S. wage disparity to globalization, specifically because of import competition from low-wage countries and employers taking advantage of a larger pool of low-wage labor, either by moving (or threatening to move) to developing countries or hiring recent immigrants.[44]

IN DEVELOPING COUNTRIES: Financial liberalization has led to financial crises that hit the poor hardest, while World Bank and IMF policies have slashed funding for social programs and favored agribusiness over small farmers. Between 1981 and 2001, the number of people living on less than $2 per day increased in every region of the developing world except East Asia.[45]

Boosting the Top

IN THE UNITED STATES: Executives of large corporations have enjoyed skyrocketing compensation as corporate profits, buoyed by success in global markets, have soared. The gap between average CEO pay and worker pay was 301 to 1 in 2003, up from 42 to 1 in 1982.[46]

IN DEVELOPING COUNTRIES: Many elites have gotten rich by snatching up state-owned enterprises at bargain rates when governments were forced to privatize. In 2003, Asia (excluding Japan) and Latin America boasted seventy-six of the world's 587 billionaires, up from only five in 1986. This doesn't even include Russian billionaires, who were nonexistent in 1986 but numbered twenty-four as of 2003.[47]

CLAIM #7

WHAT'S GOOD FOR GENERAL MOTORS IS GOOD FOR THE REST OF US

What is good for the country is good for General Motors and what's good for General Motors is good for the country.
—General Motors CEO Charles Wilson, testimony before Senate Armed Forces Committee, 1952

Corporate leaders often use a variation of Wilson's famous argument when urging public support for trade and investment liberalization policies. They claim these policies will make companies more competitive and profitable, and that these profits will trickle down to the rest of us. In Wilson's day, this argument carried some weight, since large U.S. corporations contributed far more to U.S. society through taxes and jobs than they do today. By contrast, global firms now have little national loyalty. While ever more influential politically, they provide a declining share of government revenues and jobs and are increasingly difficult for governments to regulate.

Declining Tax Burden

The most powerful U.S. corporations have combined geographic mobility with political clout to minimize their tax obligations. Since 1960, the share of federal tax revenues paid by corporations has dropped by nearly two-thirds.[48] According to the U.S. General Accounting Office, 61 percent of all U.S. corporations paid no taxes at all between 1996 and 2000.[49] This is partly due to a practice among many corporations with far-flung operations of simply recording profits in jurisdictions with low tax rates.

Share of Federal Taxes Paid by Corporations

25%	
20%	23.2%
15%	
10%	
5%	8.0%
0%	
1960	**2003**

Cutting Jobs While Boosting Sales

Today's top ten U.S. manufacturing firms combined employ far fewer people than they did thirty-five years ago, despite soaring revenues. Since 1968, world-wide employment at these firms has dropped 28 percent, while sales (adjusted for inflation) have climbed 133 percent.[50] Much of the drop in employment reflects technological advancements that automated certain jobs. This is not always a negative development, especially in the case of jobs that were danger-ous or otherwise undesirable. However, the basic point remains that leading firms have increased their economic and political clout while contributing less to society in jobs and tax revenues.

Top 10 U.S. Manufacturing Companies

Ranked by 2003 sales	1968 employees	2003 employees	1968 sales ($1,000)	2003 sales (1968 $1,000)	employ-ment % change	sales % change
Exxon Mobil*	151,000	88,300	14,091,337	38,686,082	-42	175
General Motors	757,231	325,000	22,755,403	35,500,817	-57	56
Ford Motor	415,039	327,531	14,075,100	29,848,666	-21	112
General Electric	400,000	305,000	8,381,633	24,348,938	-24	191
ChevronTexaco	241,974	61,533	5,459,771	20,493,014	-75	275
ConocoPhillips	35,359	39,000	2,106,868	18,048,993	10	757
IBM	241,974	319,273	6,888,549	16,173,290	32	132
Hewlett-Packard	13,430	142,000	268,849	13,257,304	957	4,831
Verizon Comm.	161,000	203,065	2,927,055	12,293,958	26	320
Philip Morris (Altria)	314,496	148,000	675,408	11,015,061	-53	1,531
Total	2,731,503	1,958,702	$77,629,973	$180,980,040	-28	133

* formerly Standard Oil of NJ

CLAIM #8

SWEATSHOPS ARE GOOD FOR POOR COUNTRIES; THE UNITED STATES DEVELOPED THAT WAY

My concern is not that there are too many sweatshops [in developing countries] but that there are too few. —Jeffrey Sachs, Columbia University [51]

For centuries, much of the world's manufacturing came from small facilities with dismal health and safety conditions where workers (often children) earned less than a poverty wage working long hours. Such facilities have earned the name "sweatshops." Some economists claim that such plants are an essential step toward prosperity for developing countries, pointing to the brutal working conditions that characterized much of early U.S. industrial development. However, while such exploitative practices might help corporations increase profits, they are not an inevitable element of a healthy development strategy.

There is more evidence that it was the struggles *against* sweatshops, not the sweatshops themselves, that led to improved working conditions in the United States. Many labor-union activists lost their lives or made other tremendous sacrifices to win the struggle for the minimum wage, the forty-hour work week, and other protections.

Sweatshops can trap workers in a vicious cycle of malnourishment, poor educational opportunities, and dangerous working conditions. This leads to more poverty and inequality, rather than laying the foundation for building a strong, empowered middle class and a viable democracy.

"If we pay them starvation wages— why do they need a lunch break?"

Nike on the Run

Footwear giant Nike is a prime example of a globe-trotting company constantly on the run in search of the lowest possible wages. In some cases, countries with sweatshops that produced goods for Nike and other companies experienced a rise in living standards. However, the improvements had more to do with the host governments' strategic industrial policies and the struggles of workers than sweatshop jobs.[52]

1967: Nike began manufacturing in Japan, with some limited production in the United States.

1972: When Japanese wages began improving, Nike took off for South Korea and Taiwan.

1986: As workers organized in Korea and Taiwan, Nike moved most of its production to Indonesia, China, and Thailand, where repressive regimes systematically violate worker rights.

1994: Nike started some production in Vietnam.

2003: China manufactures 38 percent of all Nike shoes, far more than any other country.

CLAIM #9

PRIVATIZATION LEADS TO BETTER SERVICES

Better management in the private sector, and its capacity to innovate, can lead to increased efficiency; this in turn should translate into a combination of better quality and lower-cost services.
—International Monetary Fund [53]

Governments can take various steps to reduce the scope for corruption— most involving privatization. . . . —World Bank [54]

For the past twenty-five years, a key demand of the World Bank and the IMF has been that developing countries seeking loans or debt relief must "privatize" or sell off government enterprises to private corporations. Thus far, more than 100 countries have privatized some or most of their state-owned companies, including everything from telecommunications and road-building to essential services like education, health care, and water.

More recently, privatization has also been promoted through trade negotiations. For example, through the General Agreement on Trade in Services, the WTO is establishing rules to open up local service markets to foreign businesses and restrict policies that interfere with the market (see Chapter IV for more on this).

The argument behind privatization is that public entities become bloated and corrupt as a result of being insulated from competition. Indeed, it is not difficult to find examples of government waste in the developing world—or, for that matter, in any country. However, when profit-driven corporations take over, they typically slash jobs, bust unions, and favor customers who can pay the most. As a result, there is growing evidence that privatization has consistently failed to deliver good quality, affordable services to the poor.

Privatization Pitfalls: Examples

Lights Out in Senegal: In return for debt relief, the government of Senegal was forced in 1999 to sell part of its electricity system to a Canadian firm. Promised investments and modernization did not materialize, and there were frequent power outages that caused an estimated 1.5 to 2 percent drop in GDP. Even though service improved after the government took back control of the system in 2001, the World Bank has continued to push for a renewed attempt at privatization. The World Bank and IMF also pushed Senegal to privatize a state company that handled the buying and marketing of groundnuts, an important food crop. As a result, less than 30 percent of the country's groundnut crop was collected, resulting in millions of dollars of lost income and a hunger crisis in rural areas.[55]

Failing Grades in Haiti: A 1999 IMF report on Haiti illustrates the institution's blind devotion to privatization. It described how Haiti had privatized 89 percent of schools and conceded that the quality of private schools was lower than public ones. Only 8 percent of private school teachers had full professional qualifications, compared to 47 percent in public schools. What did the report recommend? Further privatization.[56]

Manila's Water Woes: Under pressure from the World Bank, the Philippines' capital sold its water system to private corporations in 1997. A consortium called Manila Water composed of Filipino and British companies and the U.S.-based Bechtel corporation won the contract for the east side of the city, based on its promise of a 74 percent rate cut. By January 2003, Manila Water had jacked up rates by nearly 500 percent. The west side of the city went to Maynilad Water, a French-Filipino consortium that not only broke its rate-cut promises but also stopped making payments on its debt to the government in 2001. Maynilad announced it was abandoning the contract in 2002, and the government had to take over the system.[57]

In response to widespread protest, the World Bank and IMF have in recent years advised governments in some limited cases to maintain ownership of infrastructure while hiring private firms to manage services. However, this has done little to improve the impact of private-sector involvement on services for the poor.

Privatization and Corruption

Rather than reducing corruption, former World Bank Chief Economist Joseph Stiglitz believes that privatization has expanded opportunities for graft. "In country after country," Stiglitz writes, "government officials have realized that privatization meant that they no longer needed to be limited to annual profit skimming. By selling a government enterprise below market price, they could get a significant chunk of the asset value for themselves rather than leaving it for subsequent officeholders."[58]

Russia's privatization process is an extreme example. In the 1990s, the government used rigged auctions to sell off the country's crown jewel enterprises (including its oil industry) to political insiders at fire-sale prices. This impoverished the country while creating a class of so-called "oligarchs" that now dominate the economy. The number of Russian billionaires increased from zero in 1993 to twenty-four in 2003 (more than Japan).[59]

The image of private corporations as beacons of efficiency and ethics has been deeply tarnished by the wave of corporate scandals that has rocked the United States. Between 2001 and 2004, more than 120 U.S. executives faced criminal charges.[60] In Iraq, private firms contracted to carry out reconstruction have gone further to mar their reputations.

Halliburton in Iraq

The top recipient of Iraq reconstruction contracts, Halliburton has been associated with widespread fraud.

March 2003: Halliburton subsidiary Kellogg Brown and Root received a non-competitive contract for up to $7 billion over two years.[61]

January 2004: Defense Department audit suggested Halliburton overcharged for fuel deliveries.[62]

January 2004: Halliburton employees were caught taking $6 million in bribes.[63]

May 2004: Pentagon audit revealed Halliburton had charged $160 million for meals never served to troops.[64]

June 2004: Halliburton employees reported that the company instructed them to overcharge for their wages and abandon, rather than repair, expensive equipment.[65]

August 2004: Pentagon auditors found that Halliburton failed to account adequately for $1.8 billion in charges for feeding and housing troops.[66]

WE CAN FIGHT TERRORISM
WITH FREE TRADE

CLAIM #10

Free markets and free trade are key priorities of our national security strategy. —White House, National Security Strategy[67]

U.S. officials have argued for decades that trade liberalization promotes global security by reducing poverty and strengthening democracy. Since September 11, they have used this argument more forcefully to build support for a floundering U.S. trade agenda.

Claim #4 and other sections of this book address the negative impacts of these policies on poverty reduction. Free-trade agreements and market-opening policies are damaging to democracy in a number of ways:

- **Secrecy:** Trade negotiations are conducted behind closed doors, with little opportunity for citizen input. Although U.S. trade negotiators are required by law to consult with outsiders, official advisory committees are stacked with representatives of big business.

- **Investors Rule:** Investment provisions in trade agreements and other treaties threaten laws developed through the democratic process. Under NAFTA, for example, private foreign investors have the power to sue governments directly in secretive international tribunals over laws that might diminish their profits, including public interest regulations.

- **Weapons Proliferation:** The U.S. government has used globalization as an excuse to loosen restrictions on arms exports, arguing that U.S. weapon makers need to export more to stay globally competitive. As a result, U.S. arms exports nearly doubled between 1987 and 2000. After September 11, restrictions melted away even faster in order to reward allies in the war against terrorism, including notorious human rights abusers such as Uzbekistan and Kenya.

Globalization = Apathy and Violence

There is little evidence that globalization policies have strengthened democratic institutions in the developing world. For example, Latin America is the region that has most fully implemented reforms to lift barriers to trade and investment and privatize state enterprises. Yet according to a report by the UN Development Program, increasing poverty and inequality have coincided with growing ambivalence about democracy. According to the report:

- 54.7 percent of Latin Americans would prefer authoritarian rule over democracy if it would resolve their economic problems.
- 59 percent of Latin American political leaders said political parties are failing to fulfill their necessary roles.
- Four elected Latin American presidents were forced to quit between 2000 and 2004 due to public opposition.[68] All had supported economic globalization policies.

Rather than promoting security, pro-globalization policies have sparked massive protests that have often led to violent police crackdowns. According to the World Development Movement, ninety-six people were killed during protests in developing countries against the World Bank and IMF between 2000 and 2002.[69]

Countries where World Bank/IMF protestors were killed between 2000 and 2002:

Argentina
Bolivia
Brazil
Colombia
Costa Rica
Ecuador
Malawi
Nigeria
Papua New Guinea
Paraguay
Peru
South Africa

IV. Who's Driving Globalization

Marlboro maker Philip Morris sells over 2.6 billion cigarettes each day:
one for every man, woman, and child on earth every two days.
Each cigarette contains a blend of tobacco from as many as seventy nations.
Philip Morris's decisions shape the lives of hundreds of thousands
of tobacco farmers, workers in tobacco warehouses, buyers, shippers,
factory workers, Wall Street financiers, and Madison Avenue advertisers even
before the tens of millions of consumers light up each morning.

General Motors, Ford, and Chrysler drove the decisions that created
the interstate highway system, the development of suburbs, the atrophy
of public transport, and the development of millions of jobs in related
industries. Indeed, in the United States alone, the major car and truck firms
consume over 60 percent of the oil, 50 percent of the rubber,
65 percent of the iron, 50 percent of the carpeting, and 20 percent
of the electronics and aluminum produced in this country.[1]

These giant firms and their counterparts in other countries
are the principal drivers of the world economy. Their decisions shape
the lives of most of the world's people and the direction of every national
economy. They produce most of the world's goods and services,
finance that production, and trade more and more of it across borders.
In turn, they have steered the agendas of most governments at every level,
and they have twisted the operations of the global institutions set up
to govern the global economy to meet their interests.

This section first describes the growing power and influence
of global corporations. It then gives an overview of the international public
institutions and agreements that increasingly serve as battlegrounds
between corporations and citizens. The final section of this book offers
a road map to the growing citizen backlash.

A. PRIVATE ACTORS

1. Top Corporations

While our public institutions enact and enforce the rules of the road, large private corporations have been the principal driving force behind globalization.

The power of these global firms has grown in a number of ways. According to the United Nations, there were 7,000 transnational corporations in 1970. Today, there are 64,000, with 870,000 affiliates around the world.[2] Of these, the largest 200 firms are the dominant engines of the global economy.

The Top 200 Corporations Have Grown Faster Than the World Economy

Between 1983 and 2002, the sales and assets of the largest 200 firms outpaced world economic growth. At the same time, their economic expansion far exceeded the increase in their workforces. In 2002, the combined sales of the top 200 were the equivalent of 28.1 percent of world GDP, while their employees comprised only 0.82 percent of the world's workforce.[3]

Percent Growth (1983–2002)

Corporate vs. Country Economic Clout

The Top 100[4] (Fifty-two are corporations, only forty-eight are countries)

	Country or Corporation	GDP/sales 2002 ($mil)		Country or Corporation	GDP/sales 2002 ($mil)		Country or Corporation	GDP/sales 2002 ($mil)
1	United States	10,416,820	35	Greece	132,834	69	Hungary	65,843
2	Japan	3,978,782	36	TOYOTA MOTOR	131,754	70	HONDA MOTOR	65,420
3	Germany	1,976,240	37	GENERAL ELECTRIC	131,698	71	CARREFOUR	64,979
4	United Kingdom	1,552,437	38	Finland	130,797	72	Chile	64,154
5	France	1,409,604	39	Thailand	126,407	73	ALTRIA GROUP	62,182
6	China	1,237,145	40	Portugal	121,291	74	AXA	62,051
7	Italy	1,180,921	41	Ireland	119,916	75	SONY	61,335
8	Canada	715,692	42	MITSUBISHI	109,386	76	NIPPON LIFE INS.	61,174
9	Spain	649,792	43	MITSUI	108,631	77	MATSUSHITA ELEC.	60,744
10	Mexico	637,205	44	Iran, Islamic Rep.	107,522	78	Pakistan	60,521
11	India	515,012	45	South Africa	104,235	79	ROYAL AHOLD	59,455
12	Korea, Rep.	476,690	46	Argentina	102,191	80	CONOCOPHILLIPS	58,384
13	Brazil	452,387	47	ALLIANZ	101,930	81	HOME DEPOT	58,247
14	Netherlands	413,741	48	CITIGROUP	100,789	82	New Zealand	58,178
15	Australia	410,590	49	TOTAL	96,945	83	NESTLE	57,279
16	Russian Fed.	346,520	50	Malaysia	95,157	84	MCKESSON	57,129
17	Switzerland	268,041	51	Venezuela, RB	94,340	85	Peru	56,901
18	Belgium	247,634	52	CHEVRONTEXACO	92,043	86	HEWLETT-PACKARD	56,588
19	WAL-MART	246,525	53	Egypt, Arab Rep.	89,845	87	NISSAN MOTOR	56,041
20	Sweden	229,772	54	NIPPON TEL & TEL	89,644	88	Algeria	55,666
21	Austria	202,954	55	ING GROUP	88,102	89	VIVENDI UNIVERSAL	54,977
22	Norway	189,436	56	Singapore	86,969	90	BOEING	54,069
23	Poland	187,680	57	ITOCHU	85,856	91	ASSICURAZIONI GEN.	53,599
24	GENERAL MOTORS	186,763	58	IBM	83,132	92	FANNIE MAE	52,901
25	Saudi Arabia*	186,489	59	VOLKSWAGEN	82,204	93	FIAT	52,612
26	EXXON MOBIL	184,466	60	Colombia	82,194	94	DEUTSCHE BANK	52,133
27	Turkey	182,848	61	SIEMENS	77,205	95	CREDIT SUISSE	52,122
28	ROYAL DUTCH/SHELL	179,431	62	Philippines	77,076	96	MUNICH RE GROUP	51,980
29	BP	178,421	63	SUMITOMO	75,745	97	MERCK	51,790
30	Denmark	174,798	64	MARUBENI	72,165	98	KROGER	51,759
31	Indonesia	172,911	65	Czech Republic	69,590	99	PEUGOT	51,466
32	FORD MOTOR	163,871	66	VERIZON	67,625	100	CARDINAL HEALTH	51,136
33	Hong Kong	161,532	67	AMERICAN INT. GRP.	67,482			
34	DAIMLER CHRYSLER	141,421	68	HITACHI	67,228			

Top 200 Firms

The largest 200 global firms have become so dominant that they have begun to rival nation-states in their economic clout.

- The amount of money spent on cheap underwear and other discount goods at Wal-Mart in 2003 was more than the GDPs of 174 countries.
- Despite the cancer risk, cigarette smokers helped push Philip Morris (now Altria Group) sales in 2003 higher than the GDPs of 148 countries.
- Leaving countless boarded-up locally owned hardware stores in its wake, Home Depot grew from 200 stores to more than 1,500 in the past decade, with sales exceeding the GDPs of 147 countries.

A Note on the Numbers Sales are an imperfect indicator of corporate power. Since GDP measures value added, it would be preferable to compare country GDP to corporate value added. However, this would require corporate data not publicly available. A 2002 Belgian study attempted to estimate value added by extrapolating from a few industrial firms (they couldn't get any information on service firms, which have had some of the fastest growth rates).[5] Based on their scant data, comparing corporate value-added to countries' GDP, they found that of the top 100, corporations made up thirty-seven—still a staggering reflection of corporate power.

Is Big Necessarily Bad?

Some point out that mammoth corporations are more efficient because they can take advantage of economies of scale. Others argue that the development of new medicines and technologies requires massive investment in research that only large firms can afford. However, concern about the growing economic power of corporations is justified at a time when environmental and other public-interest regulations, as well as government oversight to control corporate behavior, are being weakened in most countries of the world. This has increased the possibilities for giant corporations to undermine democracy through excessive political influence and undercut the economic interests of the broader society through monopoly power.

No international body exists to break up global monopolies. The U.S. government has reduced its own antimonopoly activities since the post–World War II period when the American occupiers broke up the great business combines of Germany and Japan on the grounds that they were incompatible with democracy. Particularly since the 1980s, government has largely taken a hands-off approach.

2. Agro-monopolies

One of the most extreme examples of corporate concentration is in the food sector, from the seed producers to the grocers.

Globally, the top ten firms control:

- one-third of the total seed market;
- more than half of the biotech market; and
- 80 percent of the agrochemical market.[6]

In the United States, three to four firms control:

- more than 80 percent of the country's beef-packing, corn-trading, and soybean-crushing market;
- more than 60 percent of grain facilities, flour mills, and soybean trading; and
- more than 50 percent of broiler chickens and pork packing.[7]

With so few companies controlling so much of the food industry, consumers stand to lose. Giant firms can also put the squeeze on vulnerable suppliers, putting downward pressure on environmental and working conditions. Regulations and enforcement to deal with corporate concentration are woefully lacking. The relative handful of cases that have wound up in court illustrate the problem.

Price-fixing: when firms collude to set artificially high prices

One of the most notorious price-fixing scandals involved Archer Daniels Midland and several Asian firms in a scheme to set prices of lysine, a livestock feed additive. At the time, ADM produced 54 percent of U.S. lysine and ADM and three Asian companies produced 95 percent of global feed-grade lysine. A Purdue University economist estimated that the cartel overcharged producers and feed companies by $65 million–$140 million between 1992 and 1995.[8]

Monopsony: when corporations illegally drive down the prices of their suppliers

In 2004, a jury awarded nearly $1.3 billion to a group of cattle producers in a case against Tyson/IBP for manipulating the market to lower prices for suppliers. Experts for the plaintiffs argued that the company had depressed prices by an average of 5.1 percent over an eight-year period.[9] Similar suits have been filed against each of the four largest meatpackers.[10]

Monopoly: when dominant corporations manipulate prices

One case in the biotech industry involved an antitrust suit against the seed companies Seminis Vegetable Seeds Inc. and LSL Biotechnologies for entering into an agreement for the production of long-shelf-life tomatoes that allegedly reduced competition in the development and sale of vegetable seed.[11]

3. Big Pharma

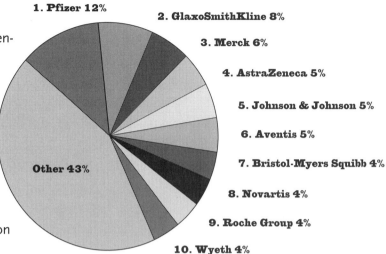

Top Ten Pharmaceutical Firms, Percent of Global Market

1. Pfizer 12%
2. GlaxoSmithKline 8%
3. Merck 6%
4. AstraZeneca 5%
5. Johnson & Johnson 5%
6. Aventis 5%
7. Bristol-Myers Squibb 4%
8. Novartis 4%
9. Roche Group 4%
10. Wyeth 4%

Other 43%

In the late 1970s, the top twenty pharmaceutical companies accounted for only 5 percent of global drug sales. Following a frenzy of mergers, the top twenty controlled more than 75 percent by 2002. The top ten firms alone now control 57 percent of the $352 billion global drug market.[12]

The pharmaceutical giants have tremendous influence over public policies that affect our lives. Although they have benefited enormously from government-funded research, they have successfully resisted most efforts aimed at ensuring that advancements in pharmaceuticals address the most pressing public-health needs. Instead, drug companies have focused on developing the most profitable products, including remedies for non-life-threatening conditions like baldness and impotence. Pfizer's Viagra sales rose 8 percent to $1.9 billion in 2002, despite the emergence of several competitors.

The power of the drug giants has made it difficult for governments to cut health costs—in poor countries as well as in the United States. For example, Swiss-based Novartis, ranked number six among global pharmaceutical firms, has blocked efforts to make its new leukemia drug, Glivec, more affordable. In Korea, the company refused to sell Glivec for the price set by the government. In 2003, after much wrangling, the government eventually agreed to a 20 percent price increase, despite angry protests by patients. In India, Novartis used Glivec as a wedge against the country's practice of authorizing generic drugs to keep costs down. Hoping to establish itself in the world's second-largest country, Novartis at first began giving away some of the drug, but canceled the program once India allowed generic versions.[13]

HOW DO CORPORATIONS EXERCISE THEIR POWER?

Most large corporations and banks maintain their own extensive lobbying operations and donate large sums to political campaigns. In addition, corporations have pooled their resources to promote globalization policies that serve their interests.

Corporate Coalitions

USA * NAFTA: Corporate America carried out one of the most expansive (and expensive) lobbying efforts in history to win passage of the North American Free Trade Agreement in 1993. The driving force was a business coalition called USA*NAFTA. Calling itself a "grassroots" organization, USA*NAFTA gave new meaning to the term by enlisting thirty-five Fortune 500 companies as "captains" to whip up support for the agreement in each of the fifty U.S. states. An army of more than 2,000 USA*NAFTA member corporations and business associations provided back-up, and contributed mightily to NAFTA's passage. During the months leading up to the vote, USA*NAFTA lobbyists wearing matching red, white, and blue neckties swarmed through Congressional office buildings and organized an exhibition of U.S. export products on the White House lawn.

ECONOMIC GROWTH AND AMERICAN JOBS COALITION: Whereas USA*NAFTA played offense, this Coalition was formed in 2004 to defend corporate America from the public outcry over foreign outsourcing of U.S. jobs. The Coalition, representing more than 200 trade groups and individual companies, is the lead opponent of legislation to restrict outsourcing of government contracts. In 2004 it helped block such legislation in more than two dozen states.

Business Associations

While the corporate coalitions tend to come and go with specific legislative campaigns, the following U.S. associations maintain a strong voice for global firms in the halls of Congress, the media, and the courts. Similar groupings can be found in other nations.

BUSINESS ROUNDTABLE: A club for the CEOs of about 150 leading U.S. firms. The Roundtable is also the driving force behind many of the campaign-oriented coalitions.

U.S. CHAMBER OF COMMERCE: The biggest business organization in the world, representing more than three million firms, the Chamber of Commerce boasted that in 2003 its lobbyists held 700 meetings with members of Congress or their aides to promote passage of trade agreements.

U.S. COUNCIL FOR INTERNATIONAL BUSINESS: Ensures that interests of global firms are heard by international agencies such as the International Labor Organization, World Trade Organization, and the Organization for Economic Cooperation and Development.

NATIONAL FOREIGN TRADE COUNCIL: Successfully sued the state of Massachusetts over a law prohibiting state agencies from purchasing goods or services from companies that do business in Burma, a notorious human rights violator. Currently working to overturn the 1789 Alien Tort Claims Act currently being used to bring charges against U.S. corporations for human-rights abuses committed overseas.

NATIONAL ASSOCIATION OF MANUFACTURERS: The nation's largest industrial trade association, representing 14,000 members and 350 member associations. Rated by *Fortune* magazine as one of the ten most influential advocacy groups.

COALITION OF SERVICE INDUSTRIES: The lead group promoting liberalization of services through trade agreements.

Corporate Think Tanks

The five major Washington-based proglobalization think tanks had combined budgets in 2003 of about $110 million. Corporate contributions comprise substantial portions of their funding and top executives and former trade negotiators figure prominently on their boards.

HERITAGE FOUNDATION: Think tank of the far right. A signature publication is the annual "Index of Economic Freedom" that ranks countries based on openness to trade and investment and other criteria.

INSTITUTE FOR INTERNATIONAL ECONOMICS: Widely cited group whose primary focus is the promotion of further trade and investment liberalization. Made rosy predictions about the benefits of NAFTA that later proved false.

AMERICAN ENTERPRISE INSTITUTE: Often referred to as the think tank of the Fortune 500. Major backer of free-trade deals. AEI received 23 percent of its revenue in 2002 from corporations.

CATO INSTITUTE: Libertarian think tank that promotes severe limits on government interference in the market. Bashes even the IMF as a market meddler.

BROOKINGS INSTITUTION: Produces pro-globalization analysis, although it has toned down its message since the late-1990s, when it published the book *Globaphobia* and had an endowed chair on international trade funded by Toyota Motor Corporation.

B. PUBLIC INSTITUTIONS

During the Great Depression of the 1930s, stock markets around the world collapsed, factories came to a grinding halt, banks went under, and trade flows collapsed as nations erected protectionist barriers. The architects of the post–World War II global economic institutions wanted, above all else, to set in place barriers against a similar collapse. Because the United States emerged from that war with as much as half the globe's measured industrial production and four-fifths of its gold reserves, U.S. negotiators were well-positioned to ensure that the rules favored continued U.S. dominance.[14]

The vision was to create public international institutions to anchor each of the three pillars of global economic activity:

- production: World Bank
- finance: International Monetary Fund
- trade: GATT, succeeded in 1995 by the WTO

British and American negotiators at a conference in Bretton Woods, New Hampshire, created the World Bank to help with reconstruction after the war and to assist long-term production in poorer countries, and the International Monetary Fund (IMF) to oversee the international financial and monetary order. The institution to free restrictions on trade, the GATT, was set up last and was replaced in 1995 by the more powerful WTO. Other public institutions have been created since World War II to supplement the activities of each of the original three, but none match the power and breadth of the World Bank, the IMF, and now the WTO.

We offer a snapshot of the three and some of their progeny, and of the moves by global corporations to twist public institutions to serve their narrow interests.

1. International Monetary Fund

The IMF was set up in 1944 to help calm financial problems around the world. In its early years, the IMF performed two important functions. First, if the price of cotton plummeted and Tanzania faced a short-term balance-of-payments crisis through no fault of its own, the IMF could rush in with short-term financing. Second, from World War II to 1971, all currencies were fixed to the U.S. dollar; the IMF helped with loans when currencies were under pressure. When the Nixon administration ended fixed exchange rates, the IMF searched for a new mission.

During the 1980s, the IMF's role shifted in two ways:

1. It focused more on ensuring that private investors and banks were shielded from large losses when their developing-country investments went bad, rather than helping governments avoid currency crises.

2. The IMF began imposing much more stringent conditions on the countries that received its loans. In the 1960s and 1970s, transnational banks had loaned hundreds of billions of dollars to poorer nations, often for giant ecology-damaging projects like dams, five-star hotels, or nuclear power plants. Much of the money lined the pockets of corrupt dictators or entrepreneurs, and by the early 1980s, much of it could not be repaid. In 1982, Mexico was the first large debtor to announce that it could not service its debts and the IMF was again brought center stage. In a series of deals with different countries, the U.S. Treasury Department and the large banks told countries that they would get no new loans (to repay the old ones) until they agreed to an IMF reform package.

Source: *A Journey Through the Global Debt Crisis,* a production of the Debt Crisis Network, 1988.

World's Financial Sheriff

If the IMF does not give its stamp of approval to a country, that government is cut off from other credit sources, including the World Bank, regional development banks, and private creditors. Thus, the IMF has tremendous leverage in pushing heavily indebted poor countries to adopt its formula for economic reform. Increasingly, the World Bank has also required similar conditions on its lending.

Unlike UN agencies, the IMF and World Bank do not operate on a "one nation, one vote" system. Instead, governance is closer to the "he who pays the piper, picks the tune" model. Countries have voting power pegged to the size of their economies (and their financial contribution to the World Bank). Accordingly, the United States and other rich nations dominate.

Most developing countries, as well as the transition countries of east and central Europe, have implemented or are in the process of implementing IMF/World Bank reforms, commonly known as "structural adjustment programs." While often succeeding in shrinking government budget deficits and eliminating hyperinflation, these policies have had a devastating impact on people, particularly women, children, and the poor. Meanwhile, the developing world's debt burden has continued to grow.

STANDARD WORLD BANK/IMF LOAN CONDITIONS

POLICY	IMPACT
reduce deficits by cutting spending	• less money for education, health care, and environment
devalue currency and export more	• acceleration of natural resource plunder for export, increased global pressures to compete by cutting prices and wages
liberalize financial markets	• more volatile short-term investment
cut price subsidies for staples	• skyrocketing prices on rice, cooking oil, and other necessities
increase interest rates to attract foreign capital	• domestic business bankruptcies, crisis for individuals with debts
privatize state-owned enterprises	• layoffs and often reduced access to services for the poor
weaken labor standards	• downward pressure on wages, working conditions

Mounting Evidence Against SAPs

Structural adjustment programs have become so unpopular that the institutions in recent years have avoided this label. The World Bank and IMF also now claim a stronger commitment to poverty reduction and require governments seeking loans and debt relief to consult with nongovernmental organizations to develop antipoverty strategies. In reality, these changes have had little effect on World Bank and IMF policies.

Zambia's Empty Schools: The Zambian government reported in February 2004 that it could not hire an additional 9,000 teachers needed to meet education goals. The problem was not a lack of resources but an IMF and World Bank cap on the percentage of the nation's GDP that could be spent on wages. If the government exceeded the limit, it would lose debt-relief benefits. Thus, while schools had been renovated, desks purchased, and teachers trained, the schools remained closed.[15]

Croatia 24/7: Although the IMF's official mandate is to promote international financial stability, it consistently meddles in unrelated matters. In Croatia, the IMF fought against a law requiring retail stores to close on Sundays and national holidays. The law was designed to protect local customs as well as reduce forced overtime work. Why did the IMF oppose it? Because it "jeopardizes free market competition . . . and GDP growth."[16]

Poverty Despite "Success": The World Bank and IMF heralded Uganda as Africa's success story after the country rapidly privatized four-fifths of its state-owned enterprises and initiated sweeping trade and investment liberalization. The institutions were so pleased that they put Uganda at the top of the list for debt relief. But the reforms did not help the poor. In fact, poverty increased from 7 to 9 million between 2000 and 2004.[17]

The IMF and the Financial Casino

In the go-go stock market boom of the 1990s, the IMF linked up with the U.S. Treasury Department to insist that more "protectionist" nations in Asia eliminate restrictions on the inflow of foreign capital. The result was an explosion of private money into Asia and the big Latin American economies. While such flows make millionaires on Wall Street and in the financial districts of Bangkok, Mexico City, and Jakarta, they also can devastate economies when economic conditions deteriorate and investors get scared. In December 1994 in Mexico, and in July 1997 in Asia, investors got spooked and billions of dollars flowed out overnight. Currencies plunged, stock markets crashed, and millions of people fell into poverty in a financial crisis with long-term effects all over the world.

In the seven years after the global crisis, the IMF made only one modest change to prevent further catastrophes: It stopped demanding that governments lift controls on capital flows. On the other hand, the IMF has not urged countries that lack controls to put them in place. The institution has taken no other significant steps to prevent future crises, such as imposing a tax on foreign exchange transactions to curb volatility or developing a coordinated system of currency exchange.

2. The World Bank

By far the largest of the public global economic institutions, the World Bank employs about 10,000 people, has offices in 109 of its 184 member nations, and routinely lends more than $20 billion a year.

World Bank loans have increasingly been tied to policy reforms similar to those required by the IMF. However, the World Bank is most known for funding "development" projects: long-term, low-interest loans for infrastructure projects like dams and power plants, and to fund agricultural "modernization." As noble as this may sound, the Bank's Articles of Agreement state as a principle goal "to promote foreign private investments." Indeed, the U.S. Treasury Department promotes U.S. government funding of the World Bank as a way to boost U.S. firms, and has claimed that for every dollar the U.S. contributes to the World Bank, U.S. corporations receive $1.30 in procurement contracts.[18]

Hence, what might have become a development institution has largely evolved into a facilitator of global corporations' overseas investments, often with devastating consequences for the environment, communities, and workers.

Major World Bank Controversies

Dams: The World Bank has financed at least 550 dams valued at $86 billion during the past sixty years. These projects have displaced at least 10 million people and often had devastating environmental effects.[19] For example, the independent World Commission on Dams found that the World Bank–financed Pak Mun Dam in Thailand resulted in a 60 to 80 percent decline in the fish catch upstream of the dam. At least fifty fish species were eliminated from the area. The loss of farming income, completely unforeseen by project designers, forced thousands of villagers to seek work in urban areas. Another 1,700 families were displaced by the dam construction.[20] World Bank lending for large dams declined after the mid-1990s, largely due to public opposition. However, in 2003, the Bank announced that it was planning to increase its funding for large infrastructure projects, including dams.

Climate Change: The World Bank has been a leading contributor to greenhouse gas emissions. The Institute for Policy Studies has calculated that between 1992 and 2003, the World Bank financed fossil fuel extraction and power plant projects that ultimately will release over 50 billion tons of carbon dioxide into the atmosphere. This is the equivalent of more than twice the amount of carbon dioxide emissions from energy consumption for the entire world in 2001. Almost every project has benefited Northern fossil fuel corporations, especially those based in the United States. The largest beneficiary has been Halliburton, the company Richard Cheney led until he became vice president of the United States in 2000.[21]

Chad-Cameroon Pipeline: In June 2000, the World Bank helped finance a $3.7 billion project to develop oil infrastructure in Chad and build an oil pipeline from that country to Cameroon's Atlantic coast. The Bank never produced a comprehensive social and environmental impact assessment, despite widespread fears of potential environmental damages such as water shortages and pollution due to oil spills. Friends of the Earth estimated that even with the most advanced technology, 2,000 gallons of oil could leak undetected from the 600-mile pipeline per day.[22] Critics also questioned why the World Bank was doing business with the notoriously corrupt government of Chad. Indeed, early on in the project, the government took $4.5 million in project revenues that it had promised to devote to poverty reduction and instead purchased weapons.[23] In general, economic benefits for the local population will be limited, since the European and U.S. companies that obtained the oil contracts are exempt from paying taxes in Chad.

Argentina's Downfall

Once touted as a model pupil of the World Bank and IMF, Argentina is now one of the strongest examples of failure.

The Argentine government has had to rely on World Bank and IMF funding to help make payments on massive debts accumulated under the country's military dictatorship. In the early 1990s, with the support of the international institutions, the country liberalized trade and financial markets and privatized virtually every public service. The IMF also supported and helped sustain a policy to peg the value of Argentina's currency to the U.S. dollar.

When the value of the U.S. dollar began to rise in the mid-1990s, Argentine exports lost competitiveness and unemployment rose. Privatization led to reduced access to services for the poor and middle class. Millions lost health coverage as private international insurers pressured providers to cut costs. Argentine banks were sold to foreign firms, which cut back lending to small and medium-sized enterprises.

In December 2001, public anger exploded in deadly riots. With the economy in free fall, Argentina declared the largest default to private banks in world history. GDP plummeted 11 percent in 2002, while unemployment rose to one-fifth of the workforce. Thousands of formerly middle class Argentines resorted to selling their possessions on the street and rummaging through garbage for food. The IMF's advice? More cuts in public spending. Only when the Argentine government threatened to default to the world's "lender of last resort" did the IMF back down. Economic growth restarted after Argentina rejected IMF advice on spending and renationalized some services.

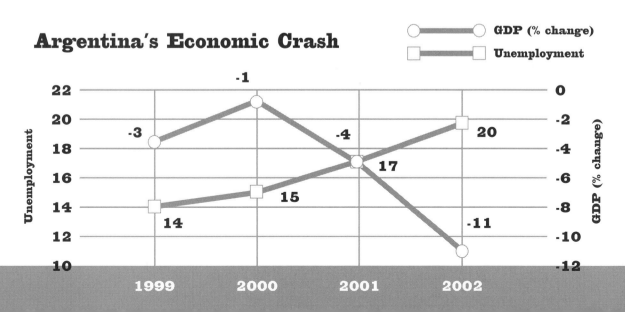

Argentina's Economic Crash

3. TRADE

World Trade Organization

More than fifty years ago, as the world began to rebuild from the ashes of World War II, a healthy and broad-based discussion emerged over the shape of a new global institution to govern trade. Government negotiators worked on the framework of a new institution, to be called the International Trade Organization. The institution was designed to balance the economic goal of liberalizing global trade with the social goal of stimulating full employment. It also set the principle that poorer nations deserved special treatment in trade in order to close the gap between rich and poor nations.

The U.S. Senate did not, however, share the same framework. It rejected the broad mandate of the proposed International Trade Organization. Instead, the world's leading nations approved a much smaller organization called the General Agreement on Tariffs and Trade (GATT). The GATT contained mechanisms to reduce barriers to trade in goods and services. It contained no measures to press for full employment or to encourage development proactively. Rather, it enshrined the concept that all countries must treat goods from all other countries on equal grounds.

Tobacco Free Trade

Just as global banks and corporations came to twist World Bank and IMF operations toward their narrow ends, so too did they deploy the GATT to break open new markets. The U.S. tobacco giants have faced a major marketing challenge as health campaigns slow the growth of cigarette sales in the United States and Western Europe. With their future tied to spreading cigarette sales in the poorer countries of the world, the companies have faced barriers in a number of nations, particularly in Asia, where governments placed restrictions on imports. Starting in the 1980s, tobacco companies went to work. With major tobacco-company contributions paving the way, the U.S. government began threatening the governments of Japan, Taiwan, South Korea, and Thailand to open their cigarette markets or face the prospect of some combination of U.S. bilateral sanctions and U.S. charges of discriminatory behavior under the GATT. A GATT tribunal ruled that Thailand must open its market, and one by one, the pressures yielded new markets to the tobacco transnationals. According to the National Bureau of Economic Research, cigarette consumption in the four Asian nations was nearly 10 percent higher in 1991 than it would have been if their markets had remained closed to U.S. cigarettes.[24]

A New Trade Era

Starting in the mid-1980s, the U.S. government began sketching plans to replace the GATT with a larger organization equipped with more powerful tools to break down barriers to trade and investment. Negotiations were completed in 1994, and the WTO replaced the GATT in 1995.

Whereas the GATT focused on reducing tariffs, the WTO also works to eliminate so-called "nontariff barriers," which can include environmental, health, and other public-interest regulations that are considered impediments to trade, as well as laws that give local firms an advantage over foreign ones. Any member country has the right to challenge other members' laws under the WTO dispute settlement process. WTO tribunals hear these cases behind closed doors in Geneva, Switzerland. If they find that a law is WTO-illegal, they have the power to order the country to change the law or face trade sanctions.

The WTO entered the public spotlight in December 1999, when tens of thousands of protestors converged on a WTO summit in Seattle, some clashing with police in an attempt to shut down the meeting. The street heat, combined with disputes between member countries, forced the organization to abandon plans to launch a new round of negotiations. The next meeting, held far from the angry crowds in isolated Doha, Qatar, concluded with plans for a new round. However, talks fell apart again in Cancún, Mexico, in 2003. As in Seattle, the streets of Cancún were filled with diverse protestors from around the world. Inside the negotiations, fighting between governments was even more intense.

Why all the controversy?

DEVELOPING COUNTRY GOVERNMENTS: In Cancún, several blocs of poorer nations led by Brazil, South Africa, India, and others rejected proposals from the richer nations for new WTO rules in several areas, including investment, primarily designed to expand opportunities for large corporations from the north. The southern governments were particularly resistant to taking on new obligations, given that promised benefits of the WTO had not yet materialized. They argued that richer nations should first do more to open their markets to goods from the south, in part by cutting agriculture subsidies that make it difficult for poor country farmers to compete.

ENVIRONMENTALISTS: The WTO's first ruling involved a successful challenge to an environmental law, the U.S. Clean Air Act. Rather than face sanctions, the U.S. government weakened a part of the Act that required foreign sources of U.S. gas imports to meet a certain cleanliness standard. Many other environmental laws have since been challenged, including U.S. dolphin and sea turtle protections, Japan's ban on fruit imports carrying invasive species, and the European Union's ban on hormone-injected beef. Technically, the WTO allows exceptions for laws that are "necessary to protect human, animal or plant life and health." However, this has proved virtually useless, since WTO tribunals have interpreted the language to mean that laws must represent the "least trade-restrictive" way to achieve the environmental goal.

LABOR UNIONS: Trade unionists made up the majority of protestors in Seattle. Around the world, unions are critical of the WTO on many grounds. They argue that the organization grants sweeping privileges to corporations while refusing to strengthen internationally recognized labor rights. And they are critical of the ongoing negotiations to lift barriers to trade and investment in services, particularly public services such as education and health care, which have been sources of decent jobs around the world.

FARMERS: In a crowd of protesters outside the WTO summit in Mexico, a South Korean farmer took his life by plunging a knife into his chest. His suicide

WTO Protest, Seattle, December 1999.

WTO protest, September 2003.

note expressed the anger of many farmers around the globe over the dumping of subsidized food in poorer countries by global corporations based in wealthier countries. He called for a global trade system that would allow poor countries to offer adequate protection to their farmers. U.S. family farm groups have also criticized the WTO for favoring large agribusiness and lowering farm incomes.

HIV/AIDS ACTIVISTS: Health activists have been among the strongest critics of the intellectual property rights rules in the WTO. These rules are designed to strengthen monopoly ownership of ideas, artistic creations, and technological innovations, including patents on life-saving medicines. In 2000, the U.S. government filed a challenge under the WTO against an effective Brazilian program that allowed the government to provide generic AIDS drugs at no cost rather than importing far more expensive drugs from United States or other foreign corporations. Under public pressure, the U.S. government withdrew the complaint. At present, there is a temporary WTO agreement that allows countries to take measures to bypass patent barriers when necessary to protect public health.

TEACHERS AND OTHER PUBLIC-SECTOR WORKERS: Teachers, health-care workers, and others concerned about public services have been critical of the WTO's General Agreement on Trade in Services (GATS). Initiated in 1995, this agreement prohibits governments from discriminating against service providers from any other member country. It also bans some government actions that are not discriminatory—for example, it puts limits on the number of service suppliers in a particular sector, even if the limits are imposed for environmental reasons. GATS negotiations are ongoing, and thus far, many countries have resisted opening up their service sectors completely. However, there are strong fears that GATS could expand or lock in the privatization of water, education, health care, and other essential services. Although U.S. officials claim that public services are excluded from GATS rules, critics charge that the treaty text is full of loopholes. For example, once a government even partly privatizes a service and places it under GATS rules, reversing this process would be difficult, since the steps necessary to curb private-sector involvement could be the target of a claim under a WTO tribunal.

Banana Split

Although WTO disputes are technically between governments, officials are usually acting as corporate proxies. Case in point: the "banana wars" between the United States and the European Union. This dispute arose over an EU policy of giving preferential treatment to bananas grown in its former Caribbean and African colonies. The United States charged that this was discriminatory against Latin American banana producers, and the WTO agreed. In 1998, when the EU refused to change the policy, the United States threatened to place 100 percent tariffs on some EU imports. Eventually, the EU backed down, in a devastating blow to small Caribbean nations dependent on banana exports. Since U.S. jobs were not at stake (no bananas are grown in the United States for export), there were strong suspicions that Chiquita, a U.S. company with extensive banana plantations in Latin America, had simply purchased the government's support. Chiquita CEO Carl Lindner and his associates had given $5 million to U.S. political campaigns between 1991 and 1998.[25]

North American Free Trade Agreement

U.S. trade officials began in the early 1990s to pursue WTO-plus agreements with smaller groupings of countries willing to go even further to lift barriers to trade and investment. As a first step, they turned to their neighbors: Canada and Mexico. The result was the North American Free Trade Agreement (NAFTA), which went into effect on January 1, 1994.

NAFTA is a huge experiment. It goes further than any other agreement in the world to lift barriers between countries with extreme gaps in living standards. In 1994, the average Mexican manufacturing wage was $2.13, compared to $13.14 for their U.S. counterparts.[26]

MEXICO

In Mexico, NAFTA supporters argued that living standards would automatically rise as the result of increased exports and foreign investment. However, in the first decade of the agreement, there has been a total disconnect between trade and wages. Mexican exports increased from $50 to $140 billion. Net foreign direct investment into Mexico also surged, from $11 billion in 1994 to $21 billion in 2001 (before dipping in the wake of September 11). Meanwhile, the value of real manufacturing wages dropped by 7 percent.[27]

Some have argued that the real key to increasing developing-country wages is productivity growth. But this has not been the case in Mexico. Between 1994 and 2000, wages fell in spite of a productivity gain of nearly 50 percent.[28]

Why the disconnect between trade and wages?

There are several factors:

LACK OF LABOR RIGHTS: A NAFTA labor side agreement has proved incapable of holding governments or corporations accountable for worker-rights violations. More than twenty complaints have been filed regarding alleged violations in all three countries, but in not a single case has the process yielded more than a bit of public exposure to the problem. In Mexico, employers routinely fire workers who try to organize independent unions.

JOB LOSSES HAVE OUTWEIGHED GAINS: While Mexico has attracted some new export jobs, global competition has contributed to widespread bankruptcy among local firms and a crisis in the countryside that has driven more rural residents to seek factory work.

Mexican Exports to U.S. and Real Manufacturing Wages (index 1994 = 100)

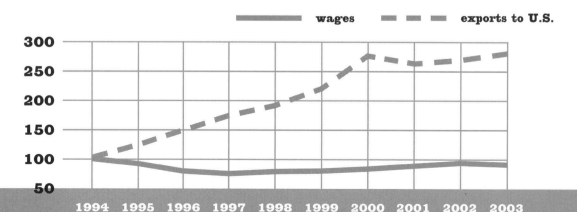

JOB FLIGHT TO CHINA: Mexico lost more than 230,000 export assembly jobs between 2000 and 2003. Analysts estimated that as much as 35 percent of these cuts were due to shifts in production to China, where wages are even lower.

UNITED STATES

In the United States, NAFTA supporters argued that the deal would lead to a net increase in high-quality U.S. jobs, as rapidly expanding exports created massive trade surpluses with Canada and Mexico. Just the opposite has occurred. Between 1994 and 2003, U.S. imports from the NAFTA partners grew far faster than U.S. exports to those countries. As a result, the U.S. trade deficit with Canada and Mexico ballooned from $13 billion to $92 billion.[29]

NAFTA Layoffs

By early 2003, the U.S. Labor Department had certified more than a half million American workers for a retraining program available to those who lose their jobs because their firm shifted production to Mexico or Canada or was hurt by competition from those countries. This number is just a fraction of total jobs lost because of the program's narrow qualification criteria. Nevertheless, these layoffs give a rough picture of who has been hit hardest. Women and people of color have been particularly affected, since they make up a disproportionate share of workers in apparel, the industry with the highest number of NAFTA-certified layoffs. Women make up 67 percent of apparel workers, while comprising only 47 percent of the

U.S. Trade Balance with Canada and Mexico

(U.S.$ million)

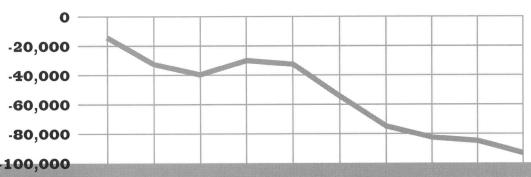

workforce. African Americans, Asians, and Latinos make up 64 percent of apparel workers, while representing only 27 percent of the total workforce.[30]

NAFTA INVESTOR RIGHTS

NAFTA's unprecedented protections for private foreign investors are perhaps the most extreme example of excessive powers granted to corporations under trade agreements. Under the pact, investors from all three countries can bypass domestic courts to sue governments directly in secretive international tribunals. This new right came with no new obligations to behave in socially responsible ways.

Over what can they sue?

Investors can demand compensation for alleged violations of a long list of investor protections. The most controversial are the protections against expropriation. In the past, this referred to government possession of a physical property, for example, taking private land to build a highway. But under NAFTA, investors are also protected against "indirect expropriation," which lawyers have interpreted to mean any government act that diminishes the value of a foreign investment—including environmental and public-health regulations.

Since NAFTA went into effect, more than thirty such suits have been filed in all three countries. These suits have sparked strong opposition from legislators and others who now must fear that laws developed through the democratic process can be threatened by expensive investor law suits.

The first NAFTA investor lawsuit was brought by the U.S.-based Ethyl Corporation over a Canadian ban on the use or sale of MMT, a gasoline additive and suspected neurotoxin. Canada responded by repealing the ban and paying the company $13 million in compensation.

International tribunals have ruled in favor of the investor (all are U.S.-based) in the following cases:[31]

Investor	Issue	Award
Metalclad	A Mexican municipality's decision to deny a permit to the firm for a hazardous waste facility in an environmentally sensitive location	Nearly $17 million
Pope and Talbot	Canada's quota system for controlling lumber exports	$580,000
S.D. Myers	A temporary Canadian ban on exports of toxic PCB wastes	$5 million
Marvin Roy Feldman Karpa	Mexico's refusal to offer rebates on cigarette export taxes	$1.5 million

As of mid-2004, the U.S. government had not yet lost a NAFTA investor case, but untold millions in U.S. taxpayer dollars have been spent defending the government against such cases, which often drag on for years. The largest suit to date was filed by Canadian-based Methanex Corporation in 1999 and was still pending as of 2004. The suit demands nearly $1 billion in compensation over a California law phasing out MTBE, a gasoline additive that has contaminated ground and surface water in the state. Another California law, this one intended to protect the environment and indigenous communities from the impacts of open-pit mining, is being challenged by a Canadian gold-mining corporation.

Free Trade Area of the Americas

In the mid-1990s, U.S. officials expressed bold plans for extending the reach of NAFTA and the WTO. In 1994, the United States, along with thirty-three other governments in the Western Hemisphere, launched negotiations around a Free Trade Area of the Americas (FTAA) that would expand the NAFTA model to include all of Latin America and the Caribbean (except Cuba). In the late-1990s, they pursued a new round of WTO negotiations that would, among other things, deepen country commitments to liberalizing investment.

NAFTA's Vicious Cycle

1. INCREASED U.S. CORN EXPORTS: During NAFTA's first seven years, U.S. corn exports to Mexico doubled.[32] On the surface, this sounds like good news for U.S. farmers and for Mexicans looking for lower prices on their staple food. The reality is more complicated.

7. U.S. AGRIBUSINESS: The firms that helped pressure Mexico to lift tariffs on U.S. corn imports under NAFTA have done very well. The profits of the two largest corn exporters, Cargill and Archer Daniels Midland, increased 28 and 233 percent in NAFTA's first ten years respectively.[39]

6. U.S. FARMERS: Despite increased exports, U.S. growers have faced the lowest corn prices in a quarter century in recent years. Although the 2002 U.S. farm bill provides billions in subsidies, about 50 percent go to the largest 10 percent of producers.[38]

2. FARMERS UPROOTED: Mexico lost 1.3 million agricultural jobs between 1993 and 2000, as peasants struggled to compete with large-scale U.S. producers.[33] Rural poverty rose from 79 to 82 percent in the first four years of NAFTA.[34]

5. U.S. BORDER: U.S. spending on immigration controls skyrocketed in NAFTA's first eight years. The number of border guards increased from about 4,000 to 9,800.[37]

4. MIGRATION PRESSURES: Poverty has driven millions to seek a better life north of the border. The number of unauthorized Mexican immigrants in the United States grew from an estimated 2 million in 1990 to 4.8 million in 2000, with a surge in growth after NAFTA went into effect.[36]

3. CONSUMERS PAY MORE: While the price paid to corn producers dropped by nearly 50 percent, the price of tortillas rose about 200 percent due to monopoly pricing.[35]

But U.S. trade officials' dreams have faced mounting resistance. The failure to launch a new round of WTO negotiations in Seattle in 1999 was only the beginning. In the FTAA talks, U.S. negotiators encountered new political leaders who were highly critical of the NAFTA-style approach. A turning point came in 2002, when Brazil elected President Luiz Inácio Lula da Silva, a former steelworker who had often called the proposed FTAA an "annexation project" of the United States. Under President Lula, the Brazilian government joined with new leaders in Argentina, Venezuela, and other countries to resist the U.S. agenda for the FTAA.

In response, the U.S. government acted in much the same way as it had in the conflict over the Iraq War in the UN Security Council. When faced with stiff resistance from some of the largest countries, it resorted to forming a so-called "coalition of the willing" with nations that for the most part were smaller and more vulnerable to U.S. pressure. In the trade arena, this has meant initiating a flurry of trade negotiations with individual or small groups of countries. The object is to create the impression of momentum behind the U.S. trade agenda and isolate what U.S. Trade Representative Robert Zoellick has called the "won't do" nations.

Coalition of the Willing on Trade

Trade Deals Initiated or Completed in 2003/2004:

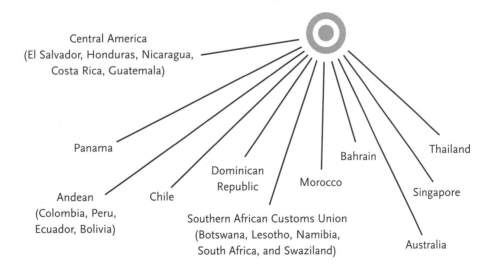

Central America (El Salvador, Honduras, Nicaragua, Costa Rica, Guatemala)

Panama

Thailand

Bahrain

Dominican Republic

Morocco

Singapore

Andean (Colombia, Peru, Ecuador, Bolivia)

Chile

Southern African Customs Union (Botswana, Lesotho, Namibia, South Africa, and Swaziland)

Australia

v. Responses to Globalization

There is no denying that the promoters of corporate-driven globalization
are a formidable force. The bulk of this book has been devoted to illustrating
the nature of their economic and political clout and examining the arguments
that they offer in their defense. But we also want to emphasize that there
is nothing inevitable about the current direction of globalization. Yes, corporations
have used their tremendous power to shape many of the rules of the road
for globalization to meet their own narrow interests. During the past two decades,
they have escalated their efforts with sweeping new rules at the local, national,
and global levels to enhance their mobility across borders.

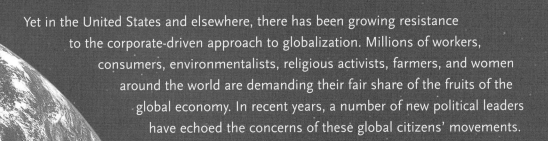

Yet in the United States and elsewhere, there has been growing resistance
to the corporate-driven approach to globalization. Millions of workers,
consumers, environmentalists, religious activists, farmers, and women
around the world are demanding their fair share of the fruits of the
global economy. In recent years, a number of new political leaders
have echoed the concerns of these global citizens' movements.

Strategies are diverse. Some attempt to stop or slow down
aspects of globalization, while others aim to reshape
its path in ways that promote democracy, equity,
and sustainability. Campaigns operate on the local,
national, and international levels. Some are
high-profile and media-driven, even involving
widely recognized global leaders and celebrities.
Others, led by the poorest of the world's poor
and in the face of extreme oppression,
operate off-camera.

Leaders Recognize the Social Impact of Globalization

KOFI ANNAN, UN Secretary-General:

Throughout much of the developing world, globalization is seen, not as a term describing objective reality, but as an ideology of predatory capitalism. Whatever reality there is in this view, the perception of a siege is unmistakable. Millions of people are suffering; savings have been decimated; decades of hard-won progress in the fight against poverty are imperiled. And unless the basic principles of equity and liberty are defended in the political arena and advanced as critical conditions for economic growth, they may suffer rejection. Economic despair will be followed by political turmoil and many of the advances for freedom of the last half-century could be lost.[1]

POPE JOHN PAUL II:

There is an economic globalization which brings some positive consequences. . . . However, if globalization is ruled merely by the laws of the market applied to suit the powerful, the consequences cannot but be negative. These are, for example, the absolutizing of the economy, unemployment, the reduction and deterioration of public services, the destruction of the environment and natural resources, the growing distance between rich and poor, and unfair competition which puts the poor nations in a situation of ever-increasing inferiority. . . .[2]

MARY ROBINSON, former president of Ireland and UN High Commissioner for Human Rights:

If the recent history of Latin America teaches anything, it is that unregulated open markets, rapid import liberalization, and the absence of essential government regulation and public services is bad for growth, bad for stability, and disastrous for poverty reduction.[3]

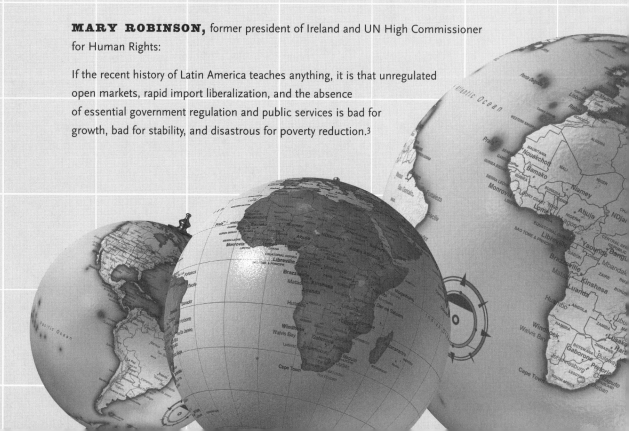

LUIZ INÁCIO LULA DA SILVA, president of Brazil:

After the 1980s, the so-called "lost decade," the 1990s was a decade of despair, brought about by a perverse model that wrongly separated the economic from the social.[4]

NELSON MANDELA, former president of South Africa:

Though international trade and investment have always been an integral part of the world economy, the extent to which all parties have benefited has depended on the circumstances in which they have taken place. The current process of globalization is no exception. . . . Fifty years ago [when the GATT was founded], few would have imagined that the exploitation of the world's abundant resources and a prodigious growth in world trade would have seen the gap between rich and poor widening.[5]

AUNG SAN SUU KYI, Nobel Peace Prize recipient and pro-democracy leader in Burma:

Until we have a system that guarantees rule of law and basic democratic institutions, no amount of aid or investment will benefit our people. Profits from business enterprises will merely go towards enriching a small, already very privileged elite.[6]

JOSEPH STIGLITZ, Nobel Economics Prize recipient and former World Bank Chief Economist:

The West has driven the globalization agenda, ensuring that it garner a disproportionate share of the benefits, at the expense of the developing world.[7]

Responding to Globalization in a Post 9-11 World

Since the September 11 tragedy, critics of globalization have faced a new challenge. Under the guise of the global "war on terrorism," authorities in the United States and other countries have taken advantage of heightened public fears to limit dissent of all types. U.S. Trade Representative Robert Zoellick, in a speech less than two weeks after the attacks, even went so far as to insinuate that there were links between the September 11 terrorists and antiglobalization protestors. "In the wake of the shock of thirteen days ago, many people will struggle to understand why terrorists hate the ideas America has championed around the world," Zoellick said. "It is inevitable that people will wonder if there are intellectual connections with others who have turned to violence to attack international finance, globalization, and the United States."[8]

Such statements have fueled harmful paranoia about demonstrations in the United States. The reality is that the overwhelming majority of activists involved in these events are peaceful. A handful have committed targeted vandalism that, while limited, has received massive, sensationalist media exposure. As of 2004, not a single person has been convicted of committing a violent act that resulted in significant bodily harm during an antiglobalization demonstration in the United States.

Police, on the other hand, have not been restrained in their use of force. During protests against the Free Trade Area of the Americas in Miami in November 2003, police fired rubber bullets and tear gas at peaceful demonstrators. Medics reported about 100 injuries inflicted by the police, including some serious head wounds. An official panel investigating police conduct during the event issued a harsh report in June 2004 stating that police had trampled on civil rights and put the city under "martial law."[9]

The Miami crackdown set a dangerous precedent for the world. In May 2004, police in Cartagena, Colombia, fired rubber bullets and tear gas at protestors, including religious leaders and a half dozen members of Congress, as they conducted a peaceful march against a proposed Andean free-trade agreement.[10] At a subsequent briefing in Washington, D.C., a Colombian government official defended the attacks, stating that American police would have responded no differently.

Despite heightened intimidation, activists have continued to mobilize around the world against the negative impacts of current globalization policies. The first section of this chapter, on People Power, highlights efforts to exert strength in numbers. At the same time, the post 9-11 climate has also encouraged a diversification of strategies, going beyond the focus on large demonstrations to utilize people's multifaceted capacities. This chapter includes just a few examples of how individuals are using their power as workers, shareholders, consumers, students, local community members, and artists to promote positive change in the global economy.

PHOTO: joy of resistance.

2,500 law-enforcement personnel were deployed to control anti-FTAA demonstrators in Miami.

A. PEOPLE POWER

World Bank and IMF

Over the past two decades, nothing has mobilized greater numbers of protestors than the World Bank and International Monetary Fund. According to the British-based World Development Movement, in 2002 alone there were more than 100 demonstrations against IMF-WB policies involving millions of people in more than twenty countries.[11] Peasant farmers, indigenous people, the unemployed, teachers, health-care workers, civil servants, religious leaders, and labor unions rallied in opposition to cuts in fiscal spending, privatization of state-run industries, and the removal of government subsidies.

© Rini Templeton

EL SALVADOR: In 2003, health-care workers and doctors carried out a nine-month strike that succeeded in blocking World Bank–supported plans to begin privatizing the nation's public health-care system. Other social sectors showed solidarity with the health workers by dressing in white and joining a demonstration of nearly 250,000 people in the capital city in October 2002.[12]

ARGENTINA: Massive protests against IMF austerity conditions forced the Argentine president to threaten to default on IMF loans in 2002. In January 2003, the IMF board, recognizing that the institution's credibility was in serious danger throughout Latin America, forced IMF management to concede to a "rollover" of Argentina's loans.

BOLIVIA: In the late 1990s, the World Bank forced Bolivia to privatize the public water system of its third-largest city, Cochabamba, by threatening to withhold debt relief and other assistance. When U.S.-based Bechtel Corporation took over the system and immediately imposed huge rate hikes on local water users, massive protests erupted, forcing the company to abandon the project. In 2003, a government proposal to develop natural gas reserves for the U.S. market via a pipeline through Chile provoked a series of general strikes and protests that drove the Bolivian president to resign.

UNITED STATES: While the largest mobilizations against the World Bank and the IMF have taken place in the debtor nations, activism in the United States has also increased in recent years. In 2000, 30,000 people demonstrated in Washington, D.C., in what was the largest protest to date at the headquarters of the World Bank and IMF. Shortly thereafter, activist groups succeeded in pressuring Congress to put new demands on the U.S. representative to the World Bank. Specifically, the law demanded that the U.S. representative oppose any loan or project that required a country to impose "user fees"—charges for basic services such as schools and health clinics. Many studies had demonstrated that such fees discourage parents from sending children to school and impoverished people of all ages from seeking health care. The law included a veiled threat to deny Congressional funding to the World Bank if the new requirement was not applied.

According to the Washington, D.C.–based 50 Years is Enough Network, a coalition formed in opposition to the World Bank and IMF, the law has had significant impacts, even if enforcement has been uneven. Within six months, the World Bank announced that it would no longer recommend or require user fees for primary education. (They continued to insist that such fees were sometimes warranted for health care.) Shortly thereafter, Tanzania announced the elimination of school fees, and over a million children who had not enrolled before started attending schools. A similar scene played out in Uganda and Kenya.

Trade Agreements

U.S. trade negotiators and corporate supporters of the trade-liberalization agenda have experienced increasing frustration in the face of mounting opposition.

Timeline of Resistance

1993: NAFTA BATTLE

In this first major trade battle, a diverse alliance of American labor, farm, environmental, and other activists joined with counterparts in Canada and Mexico to put up strong opposition to the North American Free Trade Agreement. Although supporters managed to push that deal through Congress, the struggle had only begun.

1997–2001: FAST-TRACK FAILURE

The Clinton administration tried and failed twice to obtain Congressional approval of fast-track authority—an arrangement that allows the president to negotiate new trade pacts and send them to Congress for a vote without allowing the possibility of amendment. These votes became referenda on U.S. trade policy overall, even though fast-track is a narrow procedural issue. President George W. Bush also tried and failed to muster enough support for fast-track during his first nine months in office. Then, in the aftermath of the September 11 attack, the White House took advantage of pressure on lawmakers to demonstrate unity in order to squeak out a victory on the bill—but only by a single vote in the House of Representatives.

1999: BATTLE IN SEATTLE

Opposition to the dominant approach to trade policy exploded at the Seattle summit of the World Trade Organization. In a stunning defeat for U.S. trade negotiators, the pressure of tens of thousands of protestors combined with tensions among WTO member countries from the global south to scuttle a plan for a new round of negotiations. The Seattle protests also raised the general public's awareness to an unprecedented level, as dramatic antiglobalization protest images appeared for the first time on the front pages of their newspapers and on the evening news.

2003/2004: GLOBAL TRADE MELTDOWN

In the fall of 2003, U.S. trade officials and their corporate backers were dealt a double blow. First, in September in Cancún, Mexico, a second try at launching a new WTO round collapsed. Two months later in Miami, U.S. plans for a thirty-four-country Free Trade Area of the Americas faced a severe setback.

Seattle protestor, December 1999.

Photo: Ray Lancaster, Business Representative, Plumbers, Steamfitters and Refrigeration Fitters Local.

New Political Alignments

In both the WTO and the FTAA summits, U.S. officials faced an unprecedented new alignment of developing-country leaders responding to mounting public pressure at home. In Cancún, for example, a so-called "Group of Twenty-one" including Brazil, China, India, South Africa, Egypt, and sixteen others—representing over half of the world's population—rejected U.S. and EU proposals that favored large corporations and the richer nations. Among other things, they objected to proposed rules that would prohibit governments from favoring local over global firms in public contracts, limiting the percentage of foreign ownership in domestic enterprises, and requiring foreign investors to keep some profits in the country.

Developing-country leaders argued that these rules would severely restrict their power to ensure that foreign investment benefited local people. Their resistance was stiffened when the richer nations refused to eliminate agricultural subsidies and other measures that make it more difficult for developing-country exporters to compete.

FTAA Setback

Desperate to avoid another highly visible breakdown, U.S. officials put a happy face on the situation at the 2003 Miami FTAA talks, rounding up all the trade ministers for a cheerful closing photo op. In reality, strong resistance from Brazil, Argentina, Venezuela, and to some extent from other countries left U.S. negotiators with no choice but to abandon their goal of a comprehensive, NAFTA-style agreement involving all thirty-four nations.

Activists played a critical role in throwing the FTAA off course. The Hemispheric Social Alliance, formed in 1998, united civil-society networks with the major labor federations in many countries of the Americas to oppose the trade deal and propose positive alternatives. The HSA worked with many other groups to organize teach-ins and demonstrations held parallel to the official negotiations. The largest took place in Quebec City, Canada, in 2001, where tens of thousands

converged from across the hemisphere to protest outside a ten-
foot-high security fence erected to
keep them far away from the
hemisphere's heads of state.

In the two years after the Quebec
protests, groups in many countries of the Americas carried out
consultations to give people the
opportunity to express their views

March against the FTAA, Miami, November 2003.

Photo: Jay Mallin.

on the FTAA. The most ambitious was in Brazil, where the HSA member network joined with sixty other groups, including the Brazilian Conference of
Bishops, to conduct a national referendum on the FTAA in the weeks leading
up to the fall 2002 presidential election. Ten million people participated in the
unofficial referendum, 98 percent of them voting against the FTAA.

Bridging the Divide

Prior to 2002, only one country, Venezuela, had raised strong public objections
to the FTAA. With the election of two additional Latin American presidents who
were critical of the deal (Lula in Brazil and Néstor Kirchner in Argentina),
activism around the FTAA entered a new era. No longer was there a sharp
divide between protestors outside the barricades and government officials
cloistered behind closed doors. In Miami, representatives of the Brazilian,
Argentine, and Venezuelan governments left the security zone to participate in
a public dialogue with civil society groups. Argentina's vice minister for integration encouraged the crowd: "Now is the time to multiply your efforts so the
people of the Americas have their interests defended."

Under Lula, HSA representatives were invited to join Brazil's official delegation
to negotiating sessions. As the FTAA talks continued to fall apart during 2004,
these nongovernmental participants in the negotiations freely shared information with activists throughout the hemisphere.

Positive People Power

World Social Forum

People Power is not always defensive. Beginning in 2001, tens of thousands of activists have converged annually at a World Social Forum (WSF) to share strategies and positive alternatives to current globalization policies. Initially, the WSF was designed as a counter to the World Economic Forum, an annual gathering of corporate and government leaders. While these elites gather in the posh resort town of Davos, Switzerland, the WSF has been held in developing countries. The 2004 WSF, held in Mumbai, India, drew more than 100,000 people, before returning to Porto Alegre, Brazil, in 2005. Under the slogan "Another World Is Possible," the WSF seeks to strengthen the international networks and movements working to implement alternative visions around globalization as well as militarism.

Alternative Visions

Many proponents of trade and investment liberalization policies claim that the only alternatives posed by critics are "protectionist" remedies, such as the idea of a "Fortress America" espoused by a number of right-wing critics of current trade policies. In reality, there is a wealth of creative alternative proposals that are not crudely nationalistic or antitrade. Citizens groups globally are articulating alternative platforms that do not reject all international trade and investment. But rather than being viewed as ends in themselves, trade and investment should be seen as means for promoting ideals such as equality, democracy, good jobs, a clean environment, and healthy communities. These groups' goal is to shift from an emphasis on exports based on the plunder of resources and the exploitation of workers to sustainable economic activity governed by accountable institutions.

The appendices to this book provide summaries of just two of the many collaborative projects to develop consensus around an alternative vision. The first is an effort by the International Forum on Globalization to develop a broad agenda for change that addresses the major global economic institutions and policies. The other, coordinated by the Hemispheric Social Alliance, focuses more narrowly on articulating specific recommendations for an alternative to the proposed Free Trade Area of the Americas.

B. WORKER POWER

With corporations increasingly globalized, the labor movement has also had to transcend international boundaries. Cross-border union solidarity has deep roots, dating to the early decades of this century. Since the late 1990s, a reinvigorated U.S. labor movement has increased its efforts in international solidarity work. One highlight was an innovative 1999 agreement between Cambodia and the United States to tie increased textile and apparel market access to a commitment to strengthen workers' rights protections. The U.S. government agreed to increase Cambodia's U.S. apparel quota (i.e., the volume of exports permitted into the U.S. market) in exchange for Cambodia's agreement to enforce its labor laws and abide by internationally recognized core labor standards. In addition, both parties agreed to establish a monitoring program under the International Labor Organization.

While the program is still relatively young, its first several years have seen many successes: About 40,000 Cambodian apparel workers (many young women from the countryside) have formed unions and are learning how to bargain for decent wages and working conditions. Cambodian government officials attribute this growth in unions to the quota agreement and support from the AFL-CIO's Solidarity Center, which provides training support for workers.

In addition to the AFL-CIO, a number of U.S. unions, often linked to local labor/community coalitions and other independent groups, are at the forefront of efforts to use worker power to combat the negative impacts of globalization. For example, Jobs with Justice, a labor-religious-student-community network with chapters in forty cities, has partnered with other groups to launch a Grassroots Global Justice network that links labor and other activists addressing the local impacts of globalization. The Coalition for Justice in the Maquiladoras has brought together union, religious, and other activists from the United States, Mexico, and Canada to support the struggles of workers on the U.S.-Mexico border. Other local groups like the Kansas City, Missouri–based Cross-Border Network for Justice and Solidarity, the Southwest Organizing Project, the Tennessee Economic Renewal Network, the Minnesota Fair Trade Coalition, and the New York State Labor-Religion Coalition have also promoted international solidarity actions involving labor unions and other U.S. activists.

Rio Tinto Campaign[13]

One of the most ambitious global labor initiatives has been the campaign against Rio Tinto, a British-Australian mining goliath with operations in about forty countries, including the United States.

The Rio Tinto Global Union Network was formed in 1998 in South Africa by the ICEM (International Federation of Chemical, Energy, Mine and General Workers' Union). The strategy of the network was to have local disputes drive global actions. Thus, in addition to promoting internationally recognized worker rights, the network addresses specific problems at specific mines. For example, in Australia, hundreds of Rio Tinto coal miners had been blacklisted and/or unfairly terminated, often because of their union activity. The company had reduced the workforce by 28 percent and cut real wages by 20 percent. In Brazil, the mining union was working to prevent the deaths and injuries that were occurring at a Rio Tinto gold mine where security guards were accused of shooting at people.

In 2000 and 2001, the Network organized a series of global days of action. On coordinated days with coordinated messages in multiple languages, mine workers in Australia went on strike and many demonstrations were organized in Brazil, the United States, Pakistan, and other countries, as well as at shareholder meetings in London and Australia. The company received hundreds of protest letters, and in eleven countries on four continents, Rio Tinto employees wore solidarity stickers to the workplace. The company eventually began to negotiate.

AUSTRALIA: Following the global coordinated actions, Rio Tinto agreed to stop refusing collective bargaining agreements at the Australian coal mines, and removed the local manager. Unjustly fired workers won their jobs back and/or received compensation in one of the biggest settlements in Australia's history.

BRAZIL: The local security guards were removed and the deaths and injuries stopped. The union negotiated a collective agreement at the mine for the first time and went on to organize the other two Rio Tinto mines in Brazil as well.

In addition, Rio Tinto responded to the Network's demands by changing the composition of its board to make it more independent. The Rio Tinto Global Union Network continues to campaign and struggle for the rights of Rio Tinto workers.

C. SHAREHOLDER POWER

A growing social/ethical investment movement is mobilizing the power of large institutional shareholders to exercise influence over the corporate world. The Interfaith Center for Corporate Responsibility, an association of 275 faith-based institutional investors, has been a leader of this movement for more than three decades. Every year, ICCR members sponsor more than 100 shareholder resolutions calling for socially responsible corporate policies, such as adopting internationally recognized human rights standards. Such resolutions seldom pass; however, they serve an important educational purpose and often lead to further dialogue between the investors and the corporation.

For example, the Benedictine Sisters of San Antonio, Texas, filed a shareholder resolution with Alcoa, requesting that the company pay its Mexican workers adequate wages. The resolution never even came up for a vote, but with support from ICCR and the Coalition for Justice in the Maquiladoras, two Alcoa workers were allowed to confront CEO Paul O'Neill at the company's annual meeting. At first defensive about the workers' charges of severe safety problems and poor pay, O'Neill (who later became U.S. Secretary of the Treasury) subsequently took steps to improve conditions and increase wages by 20 percent.

D. CONSUMER POWER

Consumers concerned about the current approach to globalization are increasingly speaking with their pocketbooks, both in terms of what they buy and what they do not buy.

Genetically Modified Food Fight

Consumers have allied with environmentalists and small farmers to protest genetically modified (GM) foods on every continent, uprooting crops in Britain, staging grocery-store sit-ins in Brazil, and dumping symbolic bags of corn on the steps of South Africa's parliament. The global consumer backlash against GM foods has resulted in significant legislative action:

- At least thirty-five countries have imposed limits on genetically modified food;[14]
- India, the world's second most populous country, has banned all GM seeds but cotton; and
- In the United States, governing bodies in at least seven cities and one county have either banned the growing or marketing of GM foods or called for federal labeling laws.

Consumer pressure also forced Monsanto, the largest GM seed producer, to announce in May 2004 that it was abandoning (at least temporarily) plans to commercialize the world's first GM wheat variety. However, consumers face a fierce battle with biotech firms. In 2003, Monsanto and other GM seed producers succeeded in pushing the governments of the United States, Canada, and Australia to file a challenge under the WTO over the European Union's 1998 moratorium on GM imports. In 2004, the EU began weakening its position by approving the use of a variety of GM sweet corn. Within the United States, the biotech lobby has successfully pushed state and local legislation, including at least thirty bills increasing the penalties for destroying GM crops.

Labeling Initiatives

Another consumer strategy has been to reward corporations employing "good" business practices by allowing such firms to identify their products with a label. Such activity is now advanced in such sectors as forest products, coffee, chocolate, and carpets.

BLUE ANGEL: A German labeling pioneer that began in 1977 to encourage consumers to purchase environmentally friendly products. By 2004, Blue Angel labels were found on 3,800 products.[15]

RUGMARK: Another advanced labeling effort that targets child labor in South Asia. Rugmark labels ensure that the rug was produced by adult workers, earning at least the local minimum wage. Manufacturers who join Rugmark consent to surprise inspections, while U.S. and European importers help fund the education of former child laborers. Since 1995, more than 3 million Rugmark carpets have been exported from Nepal, India, and Pakistan to Europe and North America.[16]

NO-SWEAT APPAREL: A relatively new initiative to market clothing and footwear made by unionized workers in developing countries as well as the United States.

Governments as Consumers

In 2000, the U.S. Supreme Court struck down a Massachusetts law that banned the state from giving contracts to companies that did business with Burma, one of the world's most egregious human rights abusers. The Court determined that the law conflicted with the federal government's sole right under the Constitution to make foreign policy. At the time, some feared this ruling would put an end to state and local efforts to use public-procurement laws to support international human rights. However, according to Maine-based Sweatfree Communities, five U.S. states, thirty cities, ten counties, and twenty-five public school districts have adopted procurement regulations in recent years that are designed to prevent purchases from sweatshops. Although there have been some problems with enforcement, the initiatives are a strong sign of the growing power of governments to support worker rights around the world.

Using Consumer Power to Bypass Global Corporations

Several hundred million dollars' worth of trade is now handled outside corporate channels by firms that link small-scale, often worker-owned, producer groups in developing countries directly to consumers. This "fair trade" eliminates profiteering by distributors, middlemen, and wholesalers, and often provides financing, marketing, and other skills training. The goal is to pay producers a stable price, educate consumers, and demonstrate that socially and environmentally responsible products can also be profitable. The fair-trade coffee system alone benefits over 350,000 farmers in twenty-two countries. More than 40,000 cocoa farmers are organized into eight cooperatives in eight different countries. The business generated by fair-trade organizations in Europe and the United States now accounts for only about one-tenth of one percent of all global trade, but the market is growing rapidly.

Voluntary Simplicity and Other Moves to Reduce Consumption

Growing numbers of people in the United States and other rich countries are organizing to address the very notion of consumption. In the words of Harvard economist Juliet Schor: "Americans' lives came to be organized, in a very fundamental way, around consumerism. ... Millions feel trapped in a cycle of working and spending, running faster and staying in place." Based on these precepts and on an environmental concern over the overconsumption of the earth's resources, organizations such as the Center for a New American Dream are helping people readjust their lifestyles as well as change the activities of corporations and governments that promote overconsumption.

E. STUDENT POWER

If student activism in the 1960s and 1970s focused on the Vietnam War, and in the 1980s on divestment from South Africa, the past decade will likely be remembered for the explosion of student activism around sweatshops.

United Students Against Sweatshops, founded in 1998, has chapters on more than 200 U.S. and Canadian campuses. A major focus of their work is to pressure universities to ban the purchase of products bearing the school logo from factories that violate labor rights. About 200 colleges and universities have adopted such codes of conduct. As of 2004, 124 schools were affiliated with the Workers Rights Consortium, which partners with local groups in developing countries to investigate working conditions in collegiate apparel plants.

Another initiative promoting antisweatshop codes is the Fair Labor Association, which brings together apparel firms with nongovernmental organizations advancing worker rights. The FLA grants accreditation to apparel brands like Reebok and Eddie Bauer that agree to uphold internationally recognized worker rights and allow independent monitoring of their facilities. More than 175 U.S. schools are affiliated with the FLA (including many that are also WRC affiliates).

Students have also supported the struggle of the Florida-based Coalition of Immokalee Workers to pressure Taco Bell to address abuses against workers by the company's tomato suppliers. In 2004, students at several U.S. universities carried out hunger strikes to urge their administrations to cancel Taco Bell contracts. Student power has made a difference in many cases of worker abuse. For example, in 2003, USAS protested the blacklisting of union workers at plants in El Salvador that produced clothing for Land's End. In response, six universities stopped doing business with the company. In 2004, USAS and the WRC, along with other labor organizations, helped pressure a Haitian company that made Levi's jeans to rehire workers who had been fired for carrying out a peaceful protest. Several schools in recent years have canceled contracts with Coca-Cola after students raised concerns about their treatment of workers in Colombia.

F. LOCAL POWER

Many local officials attempt to "compete" in the global economy by offering sweet deals to attract multinational, export-oriented firms to their communities. At the same time, there is growing resentment toward globe-trotting firms that:

- drain local resources to pay off distant executives and stockholders;
- use threats of plant closures to extract government subsidies and lower wages; and
- often leave in pursuit of higher profits elsewhere, leaving the community to deal with the consequences of a mass layoff.

In dozens of communities around the world, citizens are pursuing a variety of strategies to reduce the vulnerability of their local economies to the whims of global corporations. In many communities in poorer nations, local organizations of farmers and fishers are asserting control over national resources so that they can manage them sustainably. In others, such as Porto Alegre, Brazil (the site of many World Social Forums), ordinary citizens have won roles in "participatory budget" processes. Here we describe just a few efforts from U.S. communities:

Anti-Wal-Mart Campaigns

Diverse local coalitions have popped up around the country to block the entry of Wal-Mart into their communities. Complaints abound about the retail giant (particularly their mammoth Supercenters with grocery departments). Critics charge that the company exploits developing-country workers that make their products while underpaying its American retail workers, hurts smaller businesses, and contributes to traffic and other sprawl problems. The National Trust for Historic Preservation has argued that Wal-Mart megamarts threaten community character and heritage. In 2004, the group, in an effort to draw publicity to these concerns, declared the whole state of Vermont endangered because of Wal-Mart's plans to expand there.

According to Al Norman, who led a fight to keep Wal-Mart out of his own town of Greenfield, Massachusetts, in the early 1990s, more than 220 communities have blocked a "big box" store at least once. The majority of these cases involved Wal-Marts.[17] These battles typically involve disputes over zoning laws. When local officials have refused to cooperate, Wal-Mart has sometimes taken the fight directly to the people. In one highly publicized case, Wal-Mart attempted to circumvent opposition from the city council of Inglewood, California, by organizing an April 2004 ballot initiative that would have exempted the company from local zoning regulations, including environmental-impact requirements. Even though Wal-Mart outspent opponents by 10 to 1, the community overwhelmingly voted against the company.

Community and Worker Ownership

There is a growing trend toward worker and local government ownership of local enterprises. According to University of Maryland professor Gar Alperovitz, more Americans now work in firms that are partly or wholly owned by the employees than are members of unions in the private sector. In 2002, the number of firms owned by workers through employee stock-ownership plans increased to 11,000 from 4,000 in 1980. "Multinational corporations often must seek the very highest profit they can make on invested capital—whereas workers living in a community are content with substantial profits (rather than the highest possible) since the other benefits of keeping a plant in town outweigh differences in profit rates," Alperovitz explains.[18] State and local governments have also experimented with company ownership. For example, the state of Maryland provides venture capital to high-tech startups with the guarantee that the firm will stay in the state for at least five years. The program has helped create an estimated 2,500 jobs.

Local Currency

Some communities have encouraged residents to support the local economy by creating an alternative paper-money system. The most advanced "local currency" program is Ithaca HOURS, based in the small college town of Ithaca, New York. Founder Paul Glover explains, "while dollars make us increasingly dependent on multinational corporations and bankers, the HOURS reinforce community trading and expand commerce that is more accountable to our concerns for

ecology and social justice." Each HOUR is worth $10, the wage for an average hour of work. Thus, each bill is good for one hour of labor or its negotiated value in goods and services. Since 1991, organizers have issued about $105,000 worth of HOURS, and thousands of people—including 400 business proprietors—have used them in transactions worth millions of dollars.[19]

Linking Tax Breaks to Good Jobs

As corporations become ever more mobile, many state and local governments are attempting to pressure firms to create high-quality stable employment in their communities by attaching strings to tax-incentive deals. According to the nonprofit organization Good Jobs First, forty-three states, forty-one cities, and five counties now condition subsidies on job-quality standards.[20] These may include requiring the firm to create and maintain a certain number of jobs, pay workers a living wage, or provide health benefits.

G. ARTIST POWER

Visual artistry and street theater have helped globalization activists reach new audiences and transformed demonstrations into festivals of colorful and creative expression.

Puppets Imprisoned

On the eve of a major protest against the World Bank and IMF in 2000, Washington, D.C., police took actions that suggested they understand how powerful art can be. Under the questionable pretense of preventing a fire hazard, police raided an activist training center and confiscated gigantic papier-mâché puppets, including a massive smiling sun, that had been constructed for the rally.

In the face of rather embarrassing media coverage and passionate pleas for freedom, police liberated the puppets in time for the demonstration.

Beehive Collective

A decentralized group of graphic artists and educators, the Maine-based Beehive Collective is determined to "subvert the talking-head-at-the-podium approach to political discussion." Since 2000, the Collective has designed and distributed 45,000 educational posters on globalization and other issues through "pollination tours" on college campuses, high schools, community centers, and at major demonstrations. In 2003, their featured work was a portable sixteen-foot mural depicting images related to the proposed Free Trade Area of the Americas. Presenters explain the mural's details and facts, helping to break down complex issues into smaller, digestible chunks. The FTAA mural went on a road show around the country in addition to appearing at the official FTAA summit in Miami.

Music

Music can be a powerful weapon. In 1996, a song recorded by a truck driver from Buffalo, New York, helped force a Dutch retailer to the negotiating table over a dispute with U.S. workers. The company, Royal Dutch Ahold, is the largest supermarket chain in the Eastern United States. Residents in the Buffalo area were angered when the firm planned to make changes in its delivery system that would have resulted in significant job loss and threatened local family-owned grocery stores. In response to the dispute, Teamster Kelly Eddington recorded a song in his basement studio to the tune of Harry Belafonte's "Banana Boat Song," except the lyrics went "Ahold Come... and the Jobs Go Away." The song became so popular on Dutch radio that even the Ahold CEO couldn't avoid hearing it. In the end, the Teamsters and a broad coalition of community groups, backed by international support, managed to pressure the company to sign a code of conduct for its U.S. operations.[21]

Many more well-known musicians are also working to raise consciousness of globalization. In 2003, a group of diverse stars including British singer-songwriter Billy Bragg, country singer Steve Earle, Lester Chambers of the Chambers Brothers, and Tom Morello of Audioslave performed in thirteen U.S. cities to expose the negative impacts of free trade and media concentration. A highlight was an appearance at a rally in Miami against the proposed Free Trade Area of the Americas. Bragg said, "You can't change the world by singing songs. But hopefully we can encourage and inspire the activism that can."

After performing, the musicians marched with the thousands of activists who had converged on the city to protest the FTAA. Morello later told *Newsweek*, "We were proud to march shoulder to shoulder with 10,000 steelworkers and the AFL-CIO in the streets of Miami and were also proud to stand with the students and activists and anarchists in the streets as they were mowed down with tear gas."[22]

Billy Bragg performing at the anti-FTAA rally in Miami.

Bono Against Debt

U2 lead singer Bono has doggedly used his celebrity status to lobby world leaders to cancel the debts of the poorest countries. A champion of the Jubilee 2000 campaign against debt, he continues to push for further debt relief. "We can't stop until justice is done, until the poorest people in the world no longer have to repay the old and crooked debts of their great-grandfathers," Bono wrote in 2003. With fellow Irish rock star Bob Geldof, Bono is the founder of a group called DATA (Democracy, Accountability, and Transparency in Africa), which advocates for more effective policies toward the poorest continent.

Murals

The international solidarity of the U.S.-based UE union and Mexico's Authentic Labor Front (FAT) is expressed visually through murals on the unions' offices in Chicago and Mexico City. American Mike Alewitz was the principal artist on a mural entitled "Trade Unionism Without Borders" at FAT headquarters. The mural depicts workers tearing up borders imposed by bosses and features heroes from both the U.S. and Mexican labor movements. Mexican muralist Daniel Manrique created the mural at the Chicago UE office entitled "Hands in Solidarity—Hands of Freedom."

Comic Books

Cartoonists have lent their artistic skills to support educational efforts on globalization throughout the world. In this booklet by the Coalition for Justice in the Maquiladoras, illustrations of common workplace scenarios help Mexican workers learn about their labor rights so they can more effectively defend themselves against abuses by the primarily U.S.-owned corporations operating on the border.

"What are my rights on the job?"

Theater

Particularly in rural areas and where literacy rates are low, political theater has proved to be an effective way of educating and mobilizing people around globalization issues. For example, Nepali villagers gather around boomboxes in tea shops to listen to an audiocassette of a play about hydroelectric power, featuring one of Nepal's most famous comedians. Although the World Bank canceled a large-scale dam project (Arun III) in 1995 in response to opposition from Nepali and other nations' nongovernmental organizations, the debate over such projects continues. The play satirizes the World Bank's comedy of errors over Arun III, enabling the audience to laugh at the project's absurdities while raising important questions about the rights of Nepali citizens in determining the country's future development path. The tapes and complementary comic books were produced by a U.S. group, Media for International Development, in conjunction with a Nepali human rights group, INHURED. They have distributed 5,000 tapes and 3,000 comic books throughout the country.

H. LEGAL POWER

In recent years, pioneering lawyers have opened a legal avenue for holding U.S.-based corporations accountable for human-rights abuses committed abroad. The mechanism is the once-obscure 1789 Alien Tort Claims Act (ATCA), which allows foreigners to bring civil suits in U.S. courts for serious human rights crimes committed anywhere in the world. These include murder, torture, genocide, slavery, and crimes against humanity.

The International Labor Rights Fund has filed cases against a number of global firms, including ExxonMobil, Coca-Cola, and Daimler-Chrysler. In 2004, they obtained a settlement in a case against Unocal, which the ILRF had accused of participating in and profiting from crimes, including slavery and torture, committed by the government of Burma in the construction of a natural gas pipeline.

Originally created for use against pirates, the ATCA was virtually forgotten until Peter Weiss and his colleagues at the Center for Constitutional Rights used it in 1979 to initiate and win a landmark case against Paraguayan military officials for the murder of a young man. This case opened the door for ATCA cases against corporate human rights abusers. CCR is currently involved in suits against a number of global firms.

The corporate lobby and the Bush administration have lashed out at the use of ATCA against corporations. In 2004, the White House lobbied Congress to repeal the statute, while corporations turned to the Supreme Court for help. The U.S. Chamber of Commerce, U.S. Council for International Business, and the Business Roundtable (whose members include the targets of ATCA suits) filed a brief asking the U.S. Supreme Court to narrow the application of ATCA. According to ILRF, the move backfired when the Court's June 2004 ruling erased "any doubt about the validity of the ATCA for addressing egregious human rights cases."[23]

These cases still face major hurdles, including the vast armies of lawyers that corporations have deployed to fight them. Regardless of the outcome in court, however, these cases have brought tremendous exposure to corporate abuses, potentially deterring other crimes.

Conclusion

During the past dozen years, the discussions over global economic rules have moved from elite closed-door meetings to the dinner tables of ordinary families. Citizens around the globe have united to help block some new trade deals and reject World Bank and IMF policies that hurt the poor. More and more teenagers check out their clothing labels to avoid supporting sweatshops. American voters made trade policy a front-burner issue in the 2004 presidential election. Elsewhere, outrage over the current dominant policies has driven some leaders from office while catapulting others into power. With their legitimacy eroded, world economic leaders have had to resort to meeting on remote islands or behind high barriers.

Yet we cannot yet claim total victory. While the debate has shifted and legitimacy of key institutions has eroded, the global economic policies that affect our lives today have changed in only minor ways from those of a dozen years ago. Yes, defensive actions have helped prevent further expansion of the most harmful policies. But we still need to generate more progress toward a positive future for the majority of the world's population. Sadly, the beginning of this century will likely be remembered as much as a period of reckless war as a period of fresh new global economic initiatives to reduce inequality and protect the environment.

The coming years will be a critical period for citizens concerned about corporate-driven globalization to build on their strengths and successes. We hope that the facts, ideas, and strategies presented in this book will serve these movements well as they continue to press for a positive alternative vision for the global economy.

NOTES

1   University of Maryland, Program on International Policy Attitudes, "Americans in the World: Globalization Update," January 2004.

I. **What *Is* Economic Globalization?**

1   Philip Snow, *The Star Raft: China's Encounter with Africa* (New York: Weidenfeld and Nicholson, 1988).

2   See Charles Panati, *Browser's Book of Beginnings: Origins of Everything Under and Including the Sun* (Boston: Houghton Mifflin, 1984); Hans Konig, *Columbus: His Enterprise* (New York: Monthly Review, 1991); Eduardo Galeano, *Open Veins of Latin America* (New York: Monthy Review, 1973); Richard P. Tucker, "Five Hundred Years of Tropical Forest Exploitation," in Suzanne Head and Robert Heizman, eds., *Lessons of the Rain Forest* (San Francisco: Sierra Club, 1990).

3   U.S. Department of Commerce, *U.S. Global Trade Outlook 1995–2000,* (Washington, D.C.: U.S. Department of Commerce, 1995).

4   "Emerging Market" list in *The Economist* (feature in every issue), minus the BEMS and former communist countries.

5   Based on data available in United Nations Conference on Trade and Development, *Handbook of Statistics*, 1995, 2002, 2003.

6   World Bank, World Development Indicators online, http://www.worldbank.org/data/wdi2004/index.htm.

7   Based on authors' analysis of data in the United Nations Conference on Trade and Development, *Handbook of International Trade and Development Statistics 2003* (New York and Geneva: United Nations, 2003), pp. 156–159.

8   World Bank, World Development Indicators online.

9   U.S. Department of Commerce, International Trade Administration, Office of Service Industries, March 2003.

10 Scott Ehlers, "Drug Trafficking and Money Laundering," *Foreign Policy in Focus Brief*, vol. 3, no. 16, June 1998, http://www.fpif.org/briefs/vol3/v3n16lau.html.

11 Lora Lumpe, "Small Arms Trade," *Foreign Policy in Focus Brief*, vol. 3, no. 10, May 1998, http://www.fpif.org/briefs/vol3/v3n10arms.html.

12 United Nations Information Services, "UN to Target Organized Crime," Press Release No. L/32/2000, UNIS/NAF/693, August 10, 2000.

13 New Zealand Ministry of Agriculture and Forestry, "New Zealand's First Interpol Conference: Wildlife Smuggling," media release, October 14, 2003.

14 World Wildlife Fund, "While Supplies Last: The Sale of Tiger and Other Endangered Species Medicines in North America," January 1998.

15 John Feffer, ed., *Power Trip: U.S. Unilateralism and Global Strategy After September 11* (New York: Seven Stories Press, 2003), p. 73.

16 Bruce Rich, "Export Credit and Investment Insurance Agencies: The International Context," (Washington, DC: Environmental Defense Fund, March 1998).

17 Bank for International Settlements and World Bank, World Development Indicators online.

18 World Trade Organization, *Trade and Foreign Direct Investment* (Geneva: World Trade Organization, October 1996); and *UN World Investment Report, 1997* (New York and Geneva: United Nations, 1997), p. xvi.

19 World Bank, *Global Development Finance 2004* (Washington, DC: World Bank, 2004) pp. 4, 78, and OECD press release, June 28, 2004.

20 World Bank, *Global Development Finance* (Washington D.C.: World Bank, 1998), p. 3.

21 International Confederation of Free Trade Unions, ICFTU online, Web site: http://www.icftu.org, January 21, 1999.

22 Calculated by the authors based on World Bank, World Development Indicators online.

23 Robert J. Samuelson, "Global Capitalism, Once Triumphant, Is in Full Retreat," *International Herald Tribune*, September 10 1998, p. 8.

24 World Bank, *Global Development Finance 2003*, table A.42, p. 221.

25 Ann Pettifor, Bronwen Thomas, and Michela Telatin, "HIPC—Flogging a Dead Process," Jubilee Research (UK), September 2001.

26 Susan George, *The Debt Boomerang: How Third World Debt Harms Us All* (London: Pluto Press, 1992).

27 International Organisation for Migration, "Enhancing the Contribution of Migration Research to Policy-making," February 5, 2004.

28 Bureau of Economic Analysis, "U.S. International Transactions, Revised Estimates for 1974–1996," *Survey of Current Business*, July 1997, p. 46, and Bureau of Economic Analysis, "News Release: U.S. International Transactions," March 12, 2004, Table 1.

29 World Bank, *Global Development Finance 2003*, Table A.19, p. 198.

30 General Accounting Office, "Immigration Application Fees," December 30, 2003, p. 31.

31 Calculated by the authors based on World Bank, World Development Indicators online.

32 European Commission, "Net Migration," http://europa.eu.int/comm/eurostat.

II. What's *New* About the Global Economy?

1 Bureau of Economic Analysis, "Summary Estimates for Multinational Companies: Employment, Sales, and Capital Expenditures for 2002," April 16, 2004.

2 Maria Borga and William Zeile, "International Fragmentation of Production and the Intrafirm Trade of U.S. Multinational Companies," U.S. Bureau of Economic Analysis, January 22, 2004, p. 37.

3 Export data, World Bank, *World Development Report 1997*, pp. 242–43, and World Development Indicators online. Wage data: All (except China) from U.S. Department of

Labor, Bureau of Labor Statistics, "Hourly compensation costs for production workers in manufacturing in U.S. dollars," http://www.bls.gov. For China: U.S. Department of Commerce, International Trade Administration, "Expected Wages of Selected Non-Market Economy Countries: 2001 Income Data," revised September 2003.

4   Organisation for Economic Co-operation and Development, press release, June 28, 2004.

5   U.S. Department of Commerce, International Trade Administration "Expected Wages of Selected Non-Market Economy Countries: 2001 Income Data," revised September 2003; and AFL-CIO, "Section 301 Petition Before the Office of the United States Trade Representative," March 16, 2004, p. 14.

6   AFL-CIO, "Section 301 Petition Before the Office of the United States Trade Representative," March 16, 2004, p. 81.

7   Gary Clyde Hufbauer and Yee Wong, Institute for International Economics, "Trade Frictions in an Election Year," Oriental Morning Post, January 30, 2004.

8   Calculated by the authors based on U.S. Census Bureau data.

9   Boeing, "The Boeing Corporation and China," http://www.boeing.com, June 25, 2004.

10 Wal-Mart Corporation Web site, http://www.walmartstores.com.

11 "GM Plans Massive Investment in China," Associated Press, June 7, 2004.

12 Norihiko Shirouzu, "Chain Reaction—Big Three's Outsourcing Plan," Wall Street Journal, June 10, 2004.

13 "Ford invests US$1 billion in China," Chinadaily.com, October 17, 2003.

14 "GE Bets on Finance, Power in China," Reuters, October 24, 2003.

15 Coca-Cola corporation Web site, http://www.cocacola.com.

16 Ashok Deo Bardhan and Cynthia A. Kroll, "The New Wave of Outsourcing," Fisher Center for Real Estate and Urban Economics, University of California, Berkeley, Fall 2003, p. 6.

17 Saritha Rai, "India Sees Backlash Fading Over Boom in Outsourcing," New York Times, July 14, 2004.

18 Ashok Deo Bardhan and Cynthia A. Kroll, "The New Wave of Outsourcing," Fisher Center for Real Estate and Urban Economics, University of California, Berkeley, Fall 2003, p. 5.

19 Barbara Ehrenreich, "Wal-Mars Invades Earth," New York Times, July 25, 2004.

20 David Moberg, "The Wal-Mart Effect," In These Times, July 5, 2004.

21 Oxfam, "Trading Away Our Rights," February 2004.

22 Charles Fishman, "The Wal-Mart You Don't Know," Fast Company, December 2003, pp. 68–80.

23 National Labor Committee, "Toys of Misery 2004," February 2004.

24 Oxfam, "Trading Away Our Rights," February 2004.

25 Peter S. Goodman and Philip P. Pan, "Chinese Workers Pay for Wal-Mart's Low Prices," Washington Post, February 8, 2004.

26 Kenneth E. Stone, "Impact of the Wal-Mart

Phenomenon on Rural Communities,"
Iowa State University, 1997, p. 2.

27 Philip Mattera and Anna Purinton,
"Shopping for Subsidies," Good Jobs
First, May 2004.

28 Bank for International Settlements,
"Triennial Central Bank Survey,"
March 2002, Table B.1.

29 Martin Khor, "The Economic Crisis in East
Asia: Causes, Effect, Lessons,"
International Forum on Globalization,
1998, p. 2, http://www.ifg.org/khor.html.

30 Joseph Stiglitz, *Globalization and Its
Discontents* (New York: W.W. Norton &
Co., 2002), p. 99.

31 For more information, see Brian Tokar,
ed., *Gene Traders: Biotechnology, World
Trade, and the Globalization of Hunger*
(Burlington, VT: Toward Freedom, 2004).

32 Monsanto 2003 Annual Report.

III. Globalization Claims

1 The Bush Administration's Framework
for Trade Promotion Authority,
http://www.ustr.gov/tpa.pdf.

2 U.S. Census Bureau (balance of
payments basis).

3 U.S. Department of Labor, Bureau of
Labor Statistics, "Historical Employment,
B-1. Employees on nonfarm payrolls by
major industry sector."

4 Josh Bivens, "Shifting Blame for Manufacturing Job Loss," Economic Policy Institute
Briefing Paper #149, April 8, 2004.

5 Aaron Bernstein, "Welch's March to the
South," *Business Week*, December 6, 1999.

6 Ryan Fischer, "GE's Welch shares secrets,"
Times-News (Erie, PA), November 22, 1998.

7 U.S. Department of Labor, Bureau of
Labor Statistics, "Displaced Workers
Summary," August 21, 2002.

8 U.S. Department of Labor, Bureau of
Labor Statistics, "Occupational Outlook
Handbook, 2004-05 Edition" and U.S.
Census Bureau, Poverty 2003, http://
www.census.gov/hhes/poverty/threshld/
thresh03.html.

9 Sarah Anderson, Chris Hartman, et al.,
"Executive Excess 2004," Institute for
Policy Studies and United for a Fair
Economy, August 31, 2004, p. 23.

10 Kate Bronfenbrenner, "Uneasy Terrain:
The Impact of Capital Mobility on
Workers, Wages and Union Organizing,"
Report to the U.S. Trade Deficit Review
Commission, September 6, 2000,
http://www.ustdrc.gov.

11 White House News Briefing on the
2004 Economic Report of the President,
as released by the White House,
February 9, 2004.

12 Economic Policy Institute, "EPI Issue
Guide: Offshoring," 2004.

13 *New York Times*, March 1, 1992.

14 United Nations Development Program and
Stockholm Environment Institute, *China
Human Development Report 2002* (Oxford:
Oxford University Press, 2002), pp. 21–34.

15 Kevin P. Gallagher, "NACEC and
Environmental Quality: Assessing the
Mexican Experience," in *Greening NAFTA:
The Experience and Prospects of the
North American Commission for*

Environmental Cooperation, ed. John Knox and David Market (Palo Alto: Stanford University Press, 2002).

16 Ibid.

17 International Tropical Timber Organization, "Annual Review and Assessment of the World Timber Situation," 2002, p. 12.

18 World Resources Institute, "EarthTrends Country Profiles," 2003.

19 Greenpeace, "An Overview of Asian Companies, Particularly Malaysian Companies," May 1997, p. 4.

20 Michael Astor, "Brazilian Rainforest Cut Back to Make Room for Soybeans," *Washington Post,* February 8, 2004.

21 Michael Astor, "Environmentalists Blame Brazilian Beef Exports for Amazon Destruction," *Washington Post,* April 1, 2004.

22 *Congressional Record,* March 4, 2004.

23 Daniel Seligman, "Pest Invaders: The Looming Menace," Sierra Club Web site, http://www.sierraclub.org/trade/articles/pests/pest.asp.

24 Remarks to the World Bank, July 17, 2001.

25 Marc A. Miles, et al., *2004 Index of Economic Freedom: Establishing the Link Between Economic Freedom and Prosperity* (Heritage Foundation and Wall Street Journal, 2004), p. 139.

26 Dani Rodrik, "Trading in Illusions," *Foreign Policy,* March/April 2001.

27 Mark Weisbrot, Dean Baker, Egor Kraev and Judy Chen, "The Scorecard on Globalization 1980–2000: Twenty Years of Diminished Progress," Center for Economic and Policy Research, July 11, 2001.

28 World Bank, *2004 World Development Indicators,* p. 3.

29 Amy Waldman, "Debts Drive Indian Farmers to Suicide," *New York Times,* June 7, 2004.

30 UN Food and Agriculture Organization Web site, updated February 26, 2004.

31 Oxfam America, "Make Trade Fair for Central America," September 2003, p. 8.

32 Daniel T. Griswold, "The Fast Track to Freer Trade," Cato Institute Briefing Paper No. 34, 30 October, 1997.

33 Oxfam, "Europe and the Coffee Crisis: A Plan for Action," briefing paper 36, 2003.

34 T. Christian Miller and Davan Maharaj, "Coffee's Bitter Harvest," *Los Angeles Times,* October 5, 2002, p. A1.

35 All data from Steve Beckman, United Auto Workers, Washington, D.C.

36 David Dollar and Aart Kraay, "Spreading the Wealth," *Foreign Affairs,* January/February 2002.

37 Joseph Rebello, "World Bank Study Contradicts Its Free-Trade Income Theories," Dow Jones, August 23, 2002.

38 Branko Milanovic, "Can We Discern the Effect of Globalization on Income Distribution?" World Bank, September 22, 2003.

39 Robert Hunter Wade, "The Rising Inequality of World Income Distribution," *Finance and Development* (quarterly magazine of the IMF), December 2001.

40 Miguel Szekely, "The 1990s in Latin America," *Journal of Applied Economics,* vol. VI, no. 2 (November 2003): pp. 317–39.

41 Calculated by the authors based on data in World Bank, World Development

Indicators online (GDP per capita, PPP [current international $]).

42 Poverty: World Bank, *2004 World Development Indicators*, p. 3. Billionaire wealth: *Forbes*, March 15, 2004.

43 Economic Policy Institute Web site, "Change in real hourly wage for all, by education, 1973–2001."

44 Laura D'Andrea Tyson (former chair of the Council of Economic Advisers), *Washington Post*, July 9, 1997.

45 World Bank, *2004 World Development Indicators* (Washington, D.C.: World Bank, 2004), p. 3.

46 Institute for Policy Studies and United for a Fair Economy, "Executive Excess 2004," August 26, 2004.

47 *Fortune*, October 12, 1987, and *Forbes*, March 15, 2004.

48 Institute on Taxation and Economic Policy, "State Corporate Tax Disclosure: Why It's Needed," Policy Brief #16, May 2004.

49 General Accounting Office, "Tax Administration: Comparison of the Reported Tax Liabilities of Foreign- and U.S.-Controlled Corporations, 1996–2000," February 2004, p. 6.

50 Calculated by the authors based on data from *Fortune*, May 15, 1969 and *Fortune*, April 5, 2004. Note: Due to mergers that occurred after 1968, data for that year for ChevronTexaco based on Texaco; for ConocoPhillips on Phillips Petroleum; for Verizon on GTE.

51 *New York Times*, June 22, 1997.

52 All data from Jeff Ballinger, Press for Change.

53 International Monetary Fund, "Public-Private Partnerships," March 12, 2004, p. 4.

54 World Bank, *Energy Development Report 2000* (Washington, D.C.: World Bank, 2000), p. 72.

55 Dembe Moussa Dembele, "Debt and Destruction in Senegal: A Study of Twenty Years of IMF and World Bank Policies," World Development Movement, November 2003.

56 International Monetary Fund, "Haiti: Staff Report for the 1999 Article IV Consultation," September 1999, pp. 13, 15, and 20.

57 International Consortium of Investigative Journalists, *The Water Barons* (Washington, D.C.: Public Integrity Books, 2003), pp. 54–69.

58 Joseph Stiglitz, *Globalization and Its Discontents* (New York: W.W. Norton & Co., 2002), pp. 58.

59 *Forbes*, July 18, 1994 and March 15, 2004.

60 Lou Dobbs Web site, http://www.cnn.com/CNN/Programs/lou.dobbs.tonight.

61 LOGCAP Task Order 0031. Available at: http://www.halliburtonwatch.org/news/breaux_gsm.jpg.

62 Neil King, "Pentagon Auditor Requests Probe of Halliburton," *Wall Street Journal*, January 15, 2004.

63 Neil King, "Halliburton Tells Pentagon Workers Took Kickbacks to Award Projects in Iraq," *Wall Street Journal*, January 23, 2004.

64 Matt Kelley, "Pentagon to Keep Cash From Halliburton," Associated Press, May 17, 2004.

65 T. Christian Miller, "Pentagon, Ex-Workers Hit Halliburton on Oversight, Costs," *Los Angeles Times*, June 15, 2004.

66 "Halliburton Questioned on $1.8 billion Iraq Work," Reuters, August 11, 2004.

67 National Security Council, "National Security Strategy of the United States of America," September 2002, p. 23.

68 United Nations Development Program, press release, April 21, 2004.

69 World Development Movement, "States of Unrest," reports from 2000, 2001, and 2002.

IV. Who's Driving Globalization?

1   Institute for Local Self-Reliance, "The New Biological Car," *The Carbohydrate Economy* (Summer 1998), p. 4.

2   United Nations Conference on Trade and Develoment, *World Investment Report 2003* (United Nations: New York and Geneva, 2003), p. 14.

3   Calculated by the authors from data in *Fortune*, July 21, 2003, International Labor Organization, and World Bank, World Development Indicators Online. Note: U.S. banks were excluded from assets for 2002, since they were not included in 1984 surveys.

4   Calculated by the authors from data in *Fortune*, July 21, 2003, and World Bank, World Development Indicators online. Note: Firms that are more than 50 percent government-owned were excluded. GDP for Saudi Arabia is from 2001.

5   Paul De Grauwe and Filip Camerman, "How Big Are the Big Multinational Companies?," http://www.degrauwe.org, January 2002.

6   ETC Group, "Oligopoly Inc.," December 5, 2003.

7   Mary Hendrickson and William Heffernan, "Concentration in Agricultural Markets," University of Missouri, February 2002.

8   *Purdue News*, July 1999.

9   Organization for Competitive Markets, press release, February 17, 2004.

10 John R. Wilke, "How Driving Prices Lower Can Violate Antitrust Statutes," *Wall Street Journal*, January 27, 2004.

11 Jerry Heykoop and Alejandro E. Segarra, "Merger and Antitrust Issues in Agriculture," Congressional Research Service, January 10, 2001.

12 ETC Group, "Oligopoly, Inc.," December 5, 2003, p. 3, and *Multinational Monitor*, January/February 2000.

13 Stephanie Strom and Matt Fleischer-Black, "Drug Maker's Vow to Donate Cancer Medicine Falls Short," *New York Times*, June 5, 2003.

14 Jacques Gelinas, Freedom from Debt (London: Zed Books, 1998), p. 46.

15 *The Post* (Lusaka), "Government Fails to Deploy Over 9,000 Teachers," February 2004.

16 International Confederation of Free Trade Unions, "IMF Tells Croatia to Scrap Sunday Closing Law," January 7, 2004.

17 Wairagala Wakabi, "Poverty Rising in Uganda Despite Economic Growth," *East African* (Kenya), December 1, 2003.

18 Testimony of Undersecretary of the U.S. Department of the Treasury Lawrence Summers, March 27, 1995.

19 Peter Bosshard, "The World Bank at 60: A Case of Institutional Amnesia," International Rivers Network, April 2004, p. 3.

20 World Commission on Dams, "Thailand: Pak Mun Dam and Mekong/Mun River Basins," November 2000, p. 4.

21 Jim Vallette and Steve Kretzmann, "The Energy Tug-of-War: Winners and Losers in World Bank Fossil Fuel Finance," Institute for Policy Studies, April 2004, p. 2, and personal communication with Jim Vallette, July 5, 2004.

22 Friends of the Earth Web page, "Chad-Cameroon Oil Pipeline," http://www.foe.org/camps/intl/institutions/chadcameroon.htm, p. 2.

23 Ibid., p. 1.

24 Frank J. Chaoupka and Adit Laixuthai, "U.S. Trade Policy and Cigarette Smoking in Asia," National Bureau of Economic Research Working Paper 5543, April 1996.

25 David Moberg, "Going Bananas," *In These Times*, February 21, 1999.

26 U.S. Department of Labor, U.S. Bureau of Labor Statistics, May 2004.

27 Exports: U.S. Census Bureau. Wages: World Bank, "Lessons from NAFTA for Latin American and Caribbean Countries," December 2003, p. vii (Real wages in local currency based on 1% annual average decline). FDI: World Bank, World Development Indicators online.

28 Calculated by the authors based on Mexican government data.

29 U.S. Census Bureau.

30 U.S. Department of Labor, Bureau of Labor Statistics, "Household Data Annual Averages," table 18.

31 Canadian Centre for Policy Alternatives, "NAFTA Chapter 11 Investor-State Disputes," March 2003.

32 Frank Ackerman, Timothy A. Wise, et al., "Free Trade, Corn, and the Environment: Environmental Impacts of U.S.-Mexico Corn Trade Under NAFTA," Global Development and Environment Institute, Working Paper No. 03-06, Tufts University, June 2003.

33 John Audley, et al., "NAFTA's Promise and Reality," Carnegie Endowment for International Peace, November 2003, p. 20.

34 World Bank, Memorandum of the President of the International Bank for Reconstruction and Development and the International Finance Corporation to the Executive Directors on a Country Assistance Strategy Progress Report of the World Bank Group for the United Mexican States, Report No. 22147-ME.

35 Presentation by Timothy Wise, Tufts University Global Development and Environment Institute, Brookings Institution, July 15, 2004.

36 John Audley, et al., "NAFTA's Promise and Reality," Carnegie Endowment for International Peace, November 2003, p. 49.

37 INS Fact Sheet on Border Management, February 9, 1999, and Govexec.com, "Rising INS attrition rates could threaten border security," April 10, 2002.

38 Daryll E. Ray, Daniel G. De La Torre Ugarte, and Kelly J. Tiller, "Rethinking U.S.

Agricultural Policy," University of Tennessee Agricultural Policy Analysis Center, September 2003, p. 12.

39 *Hoover's Handbook 1994* and Hoovers.com, 2004.

V. Responses to Globalization

1 Address at Harvard University, September 17, 1998.

2 Address in Mexico City, January 23, 1999, excerpted in the *New York Times*, January 24, 1999.

3 Mary Robinson, "Latin America deserves better," *International Herald Tribune*, November 18, 2003.

4 From President Lula's remarks at the Summit of the Americas in Monterrey, Mexico, January 2004, quoted in Mark Engler, "Bush's Uneasy Mexican Visita," http://Tompaine.com, January 16, 2004.

5 Address to a conference to mark the fiftieth anniversary of the GATT, Geneva, Switzerland, May 1998.

6 Speech in support of the October 7–9, 1996 Free Burma Fast, Rangoon, September 1996.

7 Joseph Stiglitz, *Globalization and Its Discontents* (New York: W.W. Norton & Co., 2002), p. 7.

8 Robert B. Zoellick, U.S. Trade Representative, "American Trade Leadership: What Is at Stake," speech delivered at the Institute for International Economics, September 24, 2001.

9 Associated Press, "Draft report: Police at FTAA meetings trampled civil rights," June 3, 2004.

10 El Universal (Colombia) "Cartagena: la Policía detuvo marcha contra el TLC y agredió también a los periodistas," May 19, 2004.

11 World Development Movement, "States of Unrest III: Resistance to IMF and World Bank Policies in Poor Countries," April 2003, p. 5.

12 Personal communication with Burke Stansbury, CISPES, June 2004.

13 Based on e-mail communication with Teresa Conrow, former global coordinator for the Rio Tinto Global Union Network, July 19, 2004.

14 Mike Toner, "Biotech Wheat Plan Halted," *Atlanta Journal and Constitution*, May 11, 2004, and Friends of the Earth, "European Commission Warned Over GM Food Import," press release, May 14, 2004.

15 Blue Angel Web site, June 2, 2004, http://www.blauer-engel.de.

16 Rugmark Web site, June 22, 2004, http://www.rugmark.org.

17 Al Norman, "Victorious Secrets," available at: http://www.sprawl-busters.com/victoryz.html.

18 Gar Alperovitz, *America Beyond Capitalism: Reclaiming Our Wealth, Our Liberty, and Our Democracy* (Hoboken: Wiley, 2005), pp. 81–87.

19 Ithaca HOURS Web site, June 1, 2004, http://www.ithacahours.com.

20 Anna Purinton, "The Policy Shift to Good Jobs," Good Jobs First, November 2003, p. 1, http://www.goodjobsfirst.org/pdf/jobquality.pdf.

21 Andy Banks, "New Voice for Workers,

New Vision for Global Unionism," International Brotherhood of Teamsters (no date).

22 Brian Braiker, "Raging Against the Machine," Newsweek Web exclusive, November 26, 2004, http://msnbc.msn.com/id/3606233/.

23 International Labor Rights Fund, "Leading Human Rights Lawyer Hails Supreme Court Decision Upholding Alien Tort Claims Act," press release, June 29, 2004.

APPENDIX I

Ten Core Principles for Sustainable Societies

The following ten principles are drawn from a project by the International Forum on Globalization to articulate a broad alternative vision for global economic rules and institutions. For more, see *Alternatives to Economic Globalization: A Better World Is Possible* (Berrett-Koehler, 2004).

1. NEW DEMOCRACY: Democracy flourishes when people organize to protect their communities and rights and hold their elected officials accountable. Accountability is central to *living democracy*. The principle of new democracy means creating governance systems that give those who will bear the costs the vote when decisions are being made.

2. SUBSIDIARITY: The principle of subsidiarity recognizes the inherent democratic right to self-determination of people, communities, and nations. It respects the notion that sovereignty resides in people. Authority of more distant levels of administration is, therefore, *subsidiary* or subordinate to the authority of more local levels that allow opportunity for direct citizen engagement.

3. ECOLOGICAL SUSTAINABILITY: Economic activity has to be ecologically sustainable. The ultimate measure of long-term viability of an economic system is whether it is able to meet the genuine needs of people without diminishing the ability of future generations to meet theirs and without diminishing the natural diversity of life on earth.

4. COMMON HERITAGE: The three categories of common heritage resources are: (1) natural resources, (2) culture and knowledge, (3) public services that governments perform on behalf of all people. Common heritage resources constitute a collective birthright to be shared equitably by all, and any right to use these resources carries a corresponding moral obligation to act as their steward on behalf of all.

5. DIVERSITY: Diversity is key to the vitality, resilience, and innovative capacity of any living system. Cultural, economic, and biological diversity is essential for a healthy, sustainable, and viable community.

6. HUMAN RIGHTS: The goal of trade and investment should be to enhance the quality of life and respect core labor, social, and other rights. Governments should not only focus on civil and political rights but should also guarantee economic, social, and cultural rights to their citizens.

7. JOBS, LIVELIHOOD, AND EMPLOYMENT: Sustainable societies protect the rights of workers in the formal sector and address the livelihood needs of the greater number of people who subsist in the informal sector as well as those who have no work or are seriously underemployed.

8. FOOD SECURITY AND SAFETY: Communities and nations are stable when their people have enough food and when these nations can produce and provide their own food. Local self-reliance in food production and the assurance of healthful safe foods should be considered basic human rights.

9. EQUITY: Social justice and greater equity—among nations, within nations, between ethnic groups, between classes, and between men and women—are cornerstones of sustainable societies.

10. THE PRECAUTIONARY PRINCIPLE: When a product or practice raises potential threats to the environment or public health, even if there is scientific uncertainty, governments should have the right to take preventative actions.

APPENDIX II

Alternatives for the Americas: A Summary

This document is the result of a multi-year collaborative process to develop a detailed alternative to the proposed Free Trade Area of the Americas. The process was coordinated by the Hemispheric Social Alliance, a coalition of labor unions and networks of peasant, indigenous, women's, and other citizens groups from across the Americas committed to advancing an alternative to corporate globalization. For a complete copy of the 100-plus-page document, see http://www.art-us.org.

General Principles: Trade and investment should not be ends in themselves, but rather the instruments for achieving just and sustainable development. Citizens must have the right to participate in the formulation, implementation, and evaluation of hemispheric social and economic policies. Central goals of these policies should be to promote economic sovereignty, social welfare, and reduced inequality at all levels.

Human Rights: A common human rights agenda should form the overall framework for all hemispheric policies, and include mechanisms and institutions to ensure full implementation and enforcement. This agenda should promote the broadest definition of human rights, covering civil, political, economic, social, cultural, and environmental rights, gender equity, and rights relating to indigenous peoples and communities.

Environment: Governments should subordinate trade and investment to policies that prioritize sustainability and environmental protection. They should also have the power to channel investment to environmentally sustainable activities, reject privatization of natural resources, eliminate policies that subsidize or encourage the use of fossil-fuel energy, and use the precautionary principle in setting public policies. Natural resources must be used to serve people's basic needs, not simply as an object of market transactions.

Gender: International conventions on women's rights should be central to all hemispheric policies, and women should be ensured greater opportunities to participate in policy-making.

Labor: Hemispheric policies should guarantee internationally recognized worker rights (to be monitored by the International Labor Organization), create a fund to provide compensation to workers and communities suffering job losses, and promote the improvement of working and living standards of workers and their families.

Immigration: Governments should adhere to international conventions on migrants' rights; ensure labor rights for all workers—regardless of immigration status—and severely penalize employers that violate these rights; grant amnesty to all undocumented workers within their borders; demilitarize border zones; and support international subsidies for areas that are major exporters of labor.

Role of the State: Hemispheric policies should not undermine the ability of the nation-state to meet its citizens' social and economic needs. Nation-states should have the right to maintain public-sector corporations and procurement policies that support national development goals. The goal of national regulations on the private sector should be to ensure that economic activities promote fair and sustainable development.

Investment: Governments should have the right to screen out investments that make no net contribution to development, especially speculative capital flows. Citizen groups and all levels of government should have the right to sue investors that violate investment rules. The NAFTA mechanism that allows investors to sue governments directly should be abolished and banned from other agreements.

Finance: Foreign debts of low-income countries and the illegitimate debts of middle-income countries should be canceled. Highly indebted countries should have their debts reduced in order to avoid negative economic, social, and environmental consequences of servicing debts that have already been paid. World Bank and IMF structural adjustment programs must be abandoned, and those institutions either fundamentally restructured or replaced.

Countries should be allowed to impose capital controls and establish their own monetary and financial policies.

Intellectual Property: Governments should have the power to establish intellectual property rules that reflect their specific social, cultural, and economic contexts. This should include the right to provisions to guarantee access to essential drugs and protect biodiversity, indigenous knowledge, and traditional and farming communities. All life forms should be excluded from patentability.

Agriculture: Hemispheric policies should allow governments the right to protect or exclude staple foods from trade agreements and support the democratization of decision-making on agricultural, fishery, and environmental policies, and especially land-reform policy, by fully involving small-scale farmers.

Market Access: The current dominant principle of "national treatment," which requires governments to treat foreign investors and products no less favorably than domestic ones, severely restricts national development planning. Governments should be allowed to pursue policies to strengthen domestic demand rather than relying entirely on external markets. Governments must have sovereign rights to provide subsidies and fiscal incentives that support legitimate social interests.

Services: Basic services such as education, health care, energy, water, and other utilities should be available to all people. In order to reach this goal, those public services should not be privatized or left to the forces of so-called market rules. Governments must also develop and maintain the technical and institutional capacity to effectively regulate services.

Enforcement and Dispute Resolution: Dispute resolution and enforcement processes must be fair and democratic and focused on reducing inequalities. There should be sufficient incentives to encourage compliance so that enforcement actions can be avoided. This would involve an assessment of compliance in each country, action plans to address obstacles to compliance, and, as a last resort, the withholding of trade-agreement benefits for corporate violators and/or governments with a record of pervasive nonenforcement.

RESOURCES

The good news is that there are far too many groups doing interesting work on globalization to begin to list them all. Instead, this edition of the *Field Guide to the Global Economy* provides a select list of Web sites that serve as clearinghouses for information on particular issues, as well as links to a wide range of groups. In this Internet age, you can easily find information on other groups described in this book.

ATTAC http://www.attac.org
Multilingual site with extensive links to groups around the world.

50 Years Is Enough Network
http://www.50years.org
Links to groups challenging the World Bank and IMF.

Focus on the Global South
http://www.focusweb.org
News, analysis, and publications on globalization from developing-country perspectives.

Global Development and Environment Institute at Tufts University
http://www.ase.tufts.edu/gdae/
Features empirical research on issues related to trade and the environment.

Global Exchange
http://www.globalexchange.org
One of the most comprehensive clearinghouses for information on books, films, and other resources.

Global Rising http://www.globalrising.org
Provides links to organizations by region and issue area.

Institute for Agriculture and Trade Policy http://www.iatp.org
Information and links on environmental, agriculture, and consumer issues.

Institute for Policy Studies
http://www.ips-dc.org
Foreign Policy In Focus and Global Economy projects provide extensive information on international policies.

International Confederation of Free Trade Unions http://www.icftu.org
Links to trade-union organizations worldwide.

International Forum on Globalization
http://www.ifg.org
Site has extensive links to international groups, and book *Alternatives to Economic Globalization* includes a valuable resource section.

World Development Movement
http://www.wdm.org.uk
Provides links to organizations working on trade and debt, as well as alternative news sources.

Third World Network
http://www.twnside.org.sg/
News, analysis, and links to other groups based in the developing world.

ACKNOWLEDGMENTS

We would like to thank the Mexican union organizers, the Filipino farmers, the Bolivian water warriors, and all the other grassroots activists around the globe whose courage inspires our work. We are also indebted to our supportive community of researchers and activists in Washington, D.C. In particular, we would like to thank Peter Bakvis of the International Confederation of Free Trade Unions, and American University professor Robin Broad for their help in shaping this book. Our trade-union colleagues Chris Townsend of United Electrical, Radio and Machine Workers; Andy Banks of International Federation of Professional and Technical Engineers; and Steve Beckman of United Auto Workers also helped us connect our research with the everyday experiences of working people.

For their dogged pursuit of the facts, we thank IPS research assistants Jon Minton, Diana Alonzo, Tammy Williams, and Nikki de la Rosa. We would also like to acknowledge the generous support of IPS's Global Economy project, which made this book possible, and support by the following foundations: CS Fund, the Foundation for Deep Ecology, the Max and Anna Levinson Foundation, the Solidago Foundation, and the Veatch Program of the Unitarian Universalist Congregation at Shelter Rock. In addition, we remain indebted to those who gave invaluable help on the first edition of this book, including our colleagues Richard J. Barnet, Saul Landau, and David Ranney, and IPS interns Tammy Lyn Donohue, Phoebe Haupt, Dori Kornfeld, and Farah Nazarali.

INDEX

ALSO AVAILABLE FROM THE NEW PRESS

Doug Henwood
AFTER THE NEW ECONOMY
The Binge . . . And the Hangover That
Won't Go Away
PB, 1-56584-983-3, 304 pages
*Economist Doug Henwood scrutinizes
the 1990s and brilliantly dissects the
so-called "new economy."*

Beth Shulman
THE BETRAYAL OF WORK
HC, 1-56584-733-4, 272 pages
*How the United States turns its back
on the working poor.*

Chuck Collins and Felice Yeskel
with United for a Fair Economy
**ECONOMIC APARTHEID IN
AMERICA**
A Primer on Economic Inequality
and Apartheid
PB, 1-56584-594-3, 240 pages
*An engaging activist guide to closing
the gap between the rich and everyone
else in America.*

Medard Gabel and Henry Bruner
GLOBAL INC.
An Atlas of the Multinational
Corporation
PB, 1-56584-727-X, 176 pages with 200
full-color maps, charts, and graphs
throughout
*A unique and startling visual representa-
tion of the rise of the global corporation.*

Saskia Sassen, foreword by
K. Anthony Appiah
**GLOBALIZATION AND ITS
DISCONTENTS**
Essays on the New Mobility of People
and Money
PB, 1-56584-518-8, 288 pages with
7 black-and-white charts
*Groundbreaking essays on the new
global economy from one of the
leading experts on globalization.*

Andrew Ross
LOW PAY, HIGH PROFILE
The Global Push for Fair Labor
PB, 1-56584-893-4, 272 pages with 31
black-and-white photographs
*Anti-sweatshop activist and commentator
Andrew Ross presents case studies from
around the world to showcase the success
and strength of the fair labor movement.*

George Monbiot
**MANIFESTO FOR A NEW
WORLD ORDER**
HC, 1-56584-908-6, 288 pages
*A global perspective on the current state
of democracy, from the most realistic
utopian of our time.*

Howard Zinn
**A PEOPLE'S HISTORY
OF THE UNITED STATES**
Abridged Teaching Edition, Revised
and Updated
PB, 1-56584-826-8, 640 pages
*Zinn's original text available specifically for
classroom use, including exercises and teach-
ing materials to accompany each chapter.*

Stephen J. Rose
**SOCIAL STRATIFICATION IN
THE UNITED STATES 2000**
The New American Profile Poster:
A Book-and-Poster Set
PB, 1-56584-550-1, 48 pages with one
full-sized poster
*A book and poster set on American
comparative wealth, based on the most
recent census data.*

James Heintz, Nancy Folbre,
Center for Popular Economics
**THE ULTIMATE FIELD GUIDE
TO THE U.S. ECONOMY**
A Compact and Irreverent Guide to
Economic Life in America
PB, 1-56584-578-1, 224 pages with
illustrations, charts, tables

*An accessible, concise reference that
provides a comprehensive and informative
overview of the U.S. economy.*

William K. Tabb
UNEQUAL PARTNERS
A Primer on Globalization
PB, 1-56584-722-9, 288 pages
*An eye-opening primer on some of the less
explored aspects of globalization.*

Randy Albelda, Nancy Folbre, and the
Center for Popular Economics
THE WAR ON THE POOR
A Defense Manual
PB, 1-56584-262-6, 144 pages
*An incisive look at self-perpetuating
poverty in America.*

Lori Wallach and Patrick Woodall,
Public Citizen
**WHOSE TRADE
ORGANIZATION?**
The Comprehensive Guide to the WTO
PB, 1-56584-841-1, 416 pages
*A meticulous chronicle of how the WTO
has eroded democracy around the world.*

Studs Terkel
WORKING
People Talk About What They Do All Day
and How They Feel About What They Do
PB, 1-56584-342-8, 640 pages
*A timeless snapshot of people's feelings
about their working lives, consisting
of over 100 interviews.*

To order, call 1-800-233-4830
To learn more about The New Press
and receive updates on new titles,
visit www.thenewpress.com.